EMOTIONS OF A PHYSICIAN

Discovering the Needs of Doctors to
Understand Their Own Experiences

MARIELLA FISCHER-WILLIAMS, M.D.

GEARHART-EDWARDS PRESS

Milwaukee

Copyright © 1993 by Mariella Fischer-Williams

Published by Gearhart-Edwards Press
Box 301 5464 N. Port Washington Road
Milwaukee, Wisconsin 53217

Printed in the United States of America

Book design by Todd Hoehn

Library of Congress Cataloging-in-Publication Data

Fischer-Williams, Mariella
    Emotions of a Physician / Mariella Fischer-Williams.
    — 1st ed.
        p.   cm.
    ISBN 0-936400-02-1 (pbk.)
    1. Physicians -- Mental Health.   I. Title.
    [DNLM: 1. Emotions. 2. Physicians -- psychology -- personal narratives.   W 62 F529e 1993]
    RC451.4P5F57   1993
    610'.1'9--dc20
    DNLM/DLC
    for Library of Congress   92-075099
                                                        CIP

Contents

	Acknowledgments	iii
	Introduction	v
Chapter 1	The troubled physician	1
Chapter 2	Early motivation	16
Chapter 3	Can I accept responsibility?	23
Chapter 4	Unavoidable sadness	33
Chapter 5	The parental role	41
Chapter 6	Hierarchy, with or without support	49
Chapter 7	Anxiety is a useful quality	58
Chapter 8	Satisfaction in making the correct diagnosis	65
Chapter 9	Sublimation: can I learn to modify?	74
Chapter 10	Competitiveness	80
Chapter 11	The acceptance of change	90
Chapter 12	The lure of discovery	100
Chapter 13	Instant gratification and infant omnipotence	109
Chapter 14	Status: fashion and fluctuations	120
Chapter 15	Imagination: the gnomes and the snake	129
Chapter 16	The person and the persona	136
Chapter 17	Compromise	146

Chapter 18 *Manipulators and manipulatees*   *152*

Chapter 19 *Dependence and independence,*
            the delicate balance   *160*

Chapter 20 *Justice should be done, and justice*
            should be perceived to be done   *169*

Chapter 21 *Good advice which cannot be taken*   *177*

Chapter 22 *The parade: Can doctors be all*
            things to all people?   *187*

Chapter 23 *Addiction to medical practice*   *194*

Chapter 24 *Perennial emotions, perpetual learning*   *202*

            Bibliography   *216*

            Index   *219*

            About the Author   *222*

            About the Book Cover   *224*

Acknowledgments

Many people have helped me for this book.

Elizabeth Stroebel, Ph.D. supported me doggedly with her enthusiasm and writing skills.

Colin Wilson, author and Ian Monro, M.D., former Editor of *The Lancet* encouraged me.

Percy Werner, my husband, was the insightful critic always ready to communicate and analyze perceptively.

Judith Hubback, M.A., my sister and analytical psychologist, gave me helpful comments.

Barry Brown, M.Sc., Ph.D.; Angela Peckenpaugh, M.A.; Jack Geist, M.D.; and Kate Reed, M.L.I.S. read the manuscript and substantially aided its progress through different stages.

Becki Weiss unfailingly worked at the lay-out.

Clearly my sincere thanks are due to all the patients whom I have met over the years, and who will never know that I am thanking them.

Dedication

To Percy Werner,
my husband, who encouraged
a physician to express her emotions,
and who shows equanimity
on both sides of the Atlantic.

Introducation

What difference do the emotions of a physician make? The arrival of Health Maintenance Organisations (H.M.O.s) in the U.S. leads some people to think that interpersonal relationships between doctors and patients will become unimportant. This is not so. In many European countries national health services do not alter the fact that these personal reactions with all their emotional flavor continue with similar intensity.

Some of the stories told in this book are of medical events which took place in Scotland and England, all within the national health service. They are no different from a personal point of view from the experiences described in the United States. The practical delivery of health care varies with the changes which are necessary with time, but the acuteness of the personal experiences persists. Men and women are emotional beings. And health care improves when this is understood.

So who wants to know about the emotions of a physician?

—Those who contemplate a career in medicine and all young doctors who wish to "look before you leap."

—As a general reader are you indifferent to, or curious about, the feelings of doctors? Do you run away from, or do you like to attach yourself to, a doctor? Do you detest, despise, envy, idealise or just plain don't understand certain doctors? Do you want your doctor to consult with you on a more personal basis?

—Those who act as role models, and who are facing change on many fronts, may want to compare their ideas with mine.

There are other reasons for examining the emotions of a physician. We all have strong feelings and opinions about health and disease, pain, life and death. Some think that doctors are insufficiently sensitive to the reactions of patients, and insufficiently aware of their own feelings. Sooner or later we all come into contact with doctors. It is civilized to bring out our biases, preferences, prejudices and preconceptions. When we read the personal stories which reveal a doctor's attitude and emotions, we can usefully build bridges between the medical profession and the public.

Why did I, a physician, enjoy writing this book?

Because having found that a career in medicine opened up a varied world of worthwhile experiences, I had pleasure in describing this life. I hope that this picture encourages young men and women to be attracted to this field.

I also enjoyed imagining myself talking with the general reader who reacts to his or her doctor and, I believe, is interested in the diversity of their doctor's emotions.

A book written to open a window into the emotions that the practice of medicine arouses in doctors looks into the land of ambivalence. To illustrate what doctors learn from their patients, each chapter in the book starts with the story of a patient whom I treated, followed by an appreciation of what I learned from that person and that situation. Sometimes this was clear at the time; often the significance appeared some years later when the rush of day-to-day events no longer obscured the scene.

You, the reader, given these examples of what some doctors feel during a life-time of interacting with patients, can make definite assertions. I make only one:

If we as doctors look into our own emotions as we go through the maze of human interaction, we enrich our own experiences. When doctors are flexible and explore their own feelings, society is enriched. When individuals are enlightened, we all gain.

The reader who is intrigued by coming into contact with doctors and their emotions can explore these avenues, and will then help to build bridges between the public and the health professionals.

People may think that reasonable action, and a rationale (defined in the dictionary as: "the logical basis") is devoid of emotion. Experience teaches us that a rationale, and "reasonable" opinions are born out of fallible sensations. When we examine our emotions, the "logical" basis of our behavior is clarified.

"By starving emotions we become humorless, rigid, and stereotyped; by repressing them we become literal, reformatory and holier-than-thou; encouraged, they perfume life; discouraged, they poison it."

Dr. Joseph Collins (1866-1950 American Neurologist).

"By all means sometimes be alone; salute thyself; see what thy soul doth wear; dare to look in thy chest, and tumble up and down what thou findest there."

Wordsworth.

CHAPTER 1

The Troubled Physician

He lay dead on the sitting room carpet. He had shot himself. His wife and ten year-old daughter found him when they opened the front door. They both stood frozen with fear, holding their shopping bags. I have difficulty in visualizing the terror of the scene. Or maybe I just shy away from that kind of horror. I prefer not to think that it exists. That person was Max, a neurologist and my partner who had been sitting in the brown leather chair of the staff room the day before.

We all knew that he had been out of spirits, but none of us, including his wife, had seen the seriousness of the situation and even if we had, could we have persuaded him to seek help or psychiatric care?. Max was not really a close friend, but nevertheless we shared at breakfast conferences or on drives to medical meetings lively discussions about consciousness, epilepsy, electrical responses, and the technique of recording experiences when the brain receives and responds to stimuli. I enjoyed his stimulating approach; but herein lay the trap. These metaphysical discussions were a deceptive cloak for a troubled physician.

Here, suddenly, everything stopped, with death on the floor. Death of a colleague, and how could this have happened? What tortured Max? And what haunts me?

My colleagues and I asked the more obvious professional questions. Did he think he was unable to satisfy the demands of patients? Did he feel inadequate in keeping up with the latest medical findings? Was he fatigued with the continuous pressure of writing medical reports? Did he feel overwhelmed by the competition in the modern practice of medicine? We also asked questions of a personal nature. Did he feel the pressure to earn enough to support the home, his wife Olga and to educate his children. Were Olga and Max unable to share and find compromises between the demands of his profession and her needs? Were the inadequacies of both of their lives overlooked? He was clear-sighted in medical matters, but there was a growing pessimism about him. Perhaps what haunts me is that there are answers to these dilemmas, but doctors are often insufficiently aware of their own emotional needs, being trained by a system where patient needs appear to supersede those of the physician.

Why didn't Max listen to his inner needs?

If physicians are trained to listen and to advise patients adequately, why do we not seem to be able to listen to colleagues and to observe signs of distress both in them and in ourselves? Is it just easier to plunge ahead, answer the telephone and get on with the emergencies and the routine without all this self-observation?

Did Max feel the pressure of time?

Every day patients and physicians are confronted with a basic conflict of how to parcel out that ingredient TIME. Time-pressures are a problem for patients and physicians alike. With the daily routine of medical appointments, a common complaint of patients is that their physicians do not give them sufficient time. From the medical diagnostic point of view, a correct diagnosis is not necessarily contingent on time. On the other hand, a patient may consider that the amount of time spent in consultation indicates interest in them as a person. Physicians, however, can learn to convey focused interest in the person independent of the time spent talking with patients.

Did Max feel invulnerable?

I am reminded of the Greek myth of Icarus who thought that he was exempt from pain and consequence. He was so enamored of his power to fly with wings that, ignoring warnings, he flew too near the sun. When the sun's rays melted the wax, he fell into the sea and drowned. Physicians risk perceiving themselves as being above trouble, above health consequences. Mistakenly they may think that because they know the dangers they "can do it". With this hubris, we risk forgetting that: "Pride comes before a fall".

When Max died, I felt guilty that I had not had sufficient insight into this troubled colleague and had not attempted some intervention, although it is an unrealistic burden to assume such responsibility. It would be arrogant of me to assume that I could have prevented Max's death. My disquiet, however, came from my inability to have helped Max look at his own emotional needs. I felt inadequate when I visited Olga, sitting on the edge of her sofa.

Guilt and inadequacy arise because physicians do not open up to each other about the emotions that their medical practice induces in them. We rarely take time to reflect upon our own emotions. We are too "busy" dealing with day-to-day affairs, putting out fires, "looking after" others, to sit down and spend time on unraveling the ties that bind us fiercely to the patients. Probably physicians trained in psychiatry do so. However I, a neurologist, like most physicians with all the advantages of a classical medical education, learn self-control, which may include inappropriate control of the emotions.

Experience has now, hopefully, taught me to look under the plastic armor that cloaks many of us physicians.

With the death of a colleague like Max, it becomes imperative to re-examine the emotional needs of physicians. For Max himself, nothing more can be done. But for those remaining, time and opportunities exist. Confrontation with the finality of death is often salutory for the observers; in this instance, physicians are forced to examine their own emotional needs. Tragedy arises, whether overt or covert, if physicians are not schooled by learning from a Max's death, and if they are unwilling to face up to the possibility of their own premature mortality. A major occupational hazard of medicine is that the doctor may not attend to his or her medical emotions, those associated with the practice of medicine.

A woman colleague, who liked her patients to call her Doctor Louise, built a very large family practice through considerable sacrifice of a personal life apart from her work. Her waiting room was always crowded; the entire neighborhood knew her as a caring physician available at all hours. They brought her fresh vegetables and paper flower bouquets that their children had made for her. She delivered their babies and then their grandchildren. She was called upon at all hours of the week without apparent patient acknowledgment of a personal life apart from theirs. Few thought to ask Doctor Louise when or where she would take a holiday.

No one saw the poverty of her life as she was greeted at home only by her collie dog, when she opened the door, too tired to cook herself a meal. No one saw that the whiskey bottle was easier to reach for as solace than the telephone for personal communication. Louise did not take time off for the most basic needs of re-energizing self.

In this way the years passed; her middle age spread was taken for granted. If asked, probably everyone would say:

"She looks all right; she has her work". And her colleagues only talked shop.

One night at 2 AM, returning home from a prolonged delivery, Louise fell asleep at the wheel and drove into a stationary truck. Chronic back-ache resulted. Prolonged physical problems, persistent fatigue, insomnia, welcomed alcohol oblivion. Failing skills, undone reports, broken appointments, patient drop-off, minor auto accidents, confrontation with law enforcement, cover-up, all accentuated by fear, pride, increased isolation, and inability to seek help filled the years. With only her dog as a companion, her neighbors began to note dog smell seeping out from under the front door.

One December day Doctor Louise did not turn up at her clinic. No one had seen her. Two days passed, three days, no answer to the telephone. When the neighbors forced their way in, Louise was found on the floor unconscious, having had a stroke. Her dog was sitting up on the couch, hungry and watching anxiously.

Doctors run the risk of isolation, particularly those who "devote" themselves to their work and their patients. In her eagerness to serve, Louise did not build up a personal life outside her medical work. She isolated herself and forgot her own needs.

The balance between work and recreation is often advised to others, but over-eager doctors may forget to practice what they preach; personal life suffers, particularly when the doctor gets older. The question is how to build up our reserves with which to respond to the needs of others.

Empathizing with those who are involved in tragedy, we need to risk being hurt, but also to understand the psycho-physical impact of constantly trying to reduce other people's complaints. There is the patient's family and the "significant others" who are all involved. Their interests are often in conflict with those of the patient. Louise, like many other physicians, tried to attend to the needs of the "significant others" as well as to the central figure, the patient, "the eye of the storm." But she forgot her own needs.

Louise is an all too frequent example of how powerful human emotions within doctors are frequently suppressed, submerged, controlled, ground down and generally go unnoticed in the daily activities of medical practice.

As a young, enthusiastic doctor in a prestigious London hospital, I looked forward every morning to entering the hospital and meeting my "chief", Professor Richards. My mind would be full of medical histories read the night before, with unanswered questions on what is the cause of multiple sclerosis, or the latest treatment of meningococcal meningitis, or why do people loose consciousness with epilepsy? As young doctors, we kept anonymous ambitions to ourselves, but the race for discovery and the earnest desire to excel permeated the group standing quietly in our white coats.

We young physicians would gather in the entrance hall of the hospital, with its marble floors, waiting for the Professor in his pin-striped suit to step out of his car. Punctually he would begin the ward round, and discuss every problem at the patient's bedside. Professor Richards' logic was clear as he disentangled each symptom of the patient. He built up a frame into which the diagnosis seemed to fit so neatly that uncertainty dropped off and the next step to be taken revealed itself clearly. At the end of the ward round, Professor Richards bade us a brief polite farewell. We had a clear picture of what to do next for the patients and went to work with diligence and alacrity.

One morning in December, Professor Richards was late. No one knew why. He arrived an unbelievable half hour late, obviously sombre. His speech was more clipped than usual, monosyllabic. No one dared ask what was wrong. We spoke only bare necessities during the ward round.

He departed quicker than usual, without looking around. Something about his over-tensed neck gave me a feeling of a numb holding-in. All day I worried silently. In the evening I learned that an hour before the ward round, the Professor had received news from Canada. His son, who lived there and was also a neurologist, had committed suicide. No one knew why. No one dared to ask.

That death weighed on us with great sadness. It was not that we were unaccustomed to witnessing deaths but these could be explained by pre-existing disease. Our compensation with patients was that we had fought together in a battle for life. But the death of Professor Richards' son was another matter, maybe because it seemed a personal failure. I visualized the Professor's work of upbringing and the son's studies, academic rewards and travel to Canada, and I grieved for a troubled colleague we did not even know. Perhaps also the father felt that he had let a son down in his own chosen profession.

Now Professor Richards was left going on his same ward rounds, visibly shutting his attache case too quickly as he departed from the bed of one patient and walked stiffly on to the next.

Other colleagues were also aching to reach out to console. Our self-imposed silence reflected how we were caught in our own net of professional restraint, the expected reining-in of emotions, with the unmentioned code of "don't demonstrate". We were left with a gulf and a freeze. Unlike the death of a patient, we were unable to broach the sadness of life and death in a colleague.

I felt a sense of guilt, of undefinable confusion and ambiguity regarding the unspoken code of emotional privacy. Did I have the right or did I lack the courage to approach Professor Richards?

The only thing that I knew of his private life was that he spent his vacations fishing in Scotland, probably standing alone all day wading in a stream. How could I approach this troubled heart? How could I, a young woman, intrude with a personal remark? TRESPASSERS KEEP OUT. Medical emotions were forbidden territory.

The restraint that excludes personal emotions, the apparent need to freeze the expression of these emotions, for reasons which are often valid, is a paradox when many of the medical situations are entangled with frayed feelings.

The rarefied atmosphere of the hospital where I worked with Professor Richards excited me for medical discoveries, but alerted me to the danger of personal closure.

The troubled physician can be portrayed in a spectrum that ranges from one who is dramatically disturbed and is driven to suicide, to one who feels unfulfilled, perceiving that life could have been more beautiful. The troubled physician is not necessarily one driven to extremes.

Many of us would like to believe that the troubled physician is a case in isolation and that we are exempt, with no resemblance to those like Max or Louise.

The troubled physician is one who is fatigued, inwardly isolated, perhaps depressed, probably angry but not aware of this anger. He or she is rigid and has suppressed imagination. This individual may have unrealistic expectations and be a workaholic, competitive and with pressure of time. Being obsessive/compulsive and with greed for money may be a substitute for inner satisfaction. These doctors deny their needs and their emotions.

Paradoxically, many of the contributing factors to these characteristics are good qualities, including the need for accuracy of problem-solving, with perseverance amounting to difficulty in letting go, and a sense of worth which is necessary for rapid decision-making. Self-reliance is a sustaining quality which can be passed on to the patient with benefit. A doctor's need, however, for recognition and admiration easily leads to self-importance. Authority, competence and power can be seductive. There is a David and Goliath syndrome of "I can do it", with the physician fighting against the odds of the patient's sickness and disaster.

Many factors lead to self-destruction in doctors, often manifested by alcohol and other drug or substance abuse, destroying the subject and the whole family.

Less obviously, if a physician suppresses and neglects personal skills outside the field of medicine, those skills atrophy. Thus frustrated, a doctor may react and "take it out" on his patients and his family. Divorce commonly results. Denial prevents this discontented physician from shedding the protective armor that medical training gives a young doctor.

Often the physician's excuse is lack of time, and when this is carried to the point of denial of needs, a doctor may take on a "poor me" attitude with a martyr syndrome. Or we have the image of a hero, irreplaceable and in great demand. The "always busy" doctor can avoid painful introspection; it is usually easier to "fix" someone else than oneself. Devotion or "addiction" to medicine can lead to family neglect. I remember the heart-rending cry of an alcoholic teen-ager: "If my father had given one-tenth of the time to me that he gave his patients, I would not be like this!"

If medical emotions, the emotions aroused by the practice of medicine, are examined throughout one's career, these problems are avoided and we can then say: "It is a good life."

Many previous biographers describe doctors, medical explorers, discoverers, teachers, surgeons and bedside physicians as generally feeling great satisfaction in their profession. On the other hand, contemporary books are now written about and by doctors who are worried, criticized and critical of the profession (see bibliography: Lipp, Katz, Alsop, Illich, Nouwen, Selzer, Patterson, Hayes). There has been a turn-around in the past twenty years or so to acknowledge the existence of the troubled physician.

Martin Lipp, M.D. in his moving book *The Bitter Pill: Doctors, Patients and Failed Expectations*, describes the suicide of a colleague, a psychiatrist. After that suicide, his colleagues gathered to give their friend a diagnosis. Dr.

Lipp wrote: "They said: 'he had pathological idealism' whatever that is." Dr. Lipp found it very sad that some people should consider idealism to be pathological, meaning "ill". I agree with Dr. Lipp. However, idealism is a complex emotion, a double-edged sword. We wish it to inspire us to devotion and hard work, but if tainted with rigidity and a power-complex, it can be destructive.

Dr. Lipp depicts the widespread depression and frustration of psychiatrists in the present system of health care in the U.S.A. A good part of the treatment of this sad situation is to re-examine the human involvement that doctors have with their patients throughout their medical lifetime. This involvement is complex.

A barrier, a disconnection, a detachment may prevent us from integrating our personalities with our professional duties. We need to prevent this barrier from building up over the years. Sometimes, however, this detachment is a protective shield desired by both doctor and patients plus their families to prevent "catastrophizing" a situation. A proper balance can be found if we stay clear-minded.

There is a crisis in medical care in the Western world. Physicians acknowledge that the doctor-patient decision-making is flawed, and the technology of medicine is insufficiently wedded to the art of personal contact. Also, because the physical aspects are insufficiently integrated with the psychological, both doctor and patient become dehumanized. Some of these problems may arise through socio-political changes in the delivery of health care and will not be considered here. Instead, by describing the satisfaction of the challenge inherent in the practice of medicine, I offer some solutions.

This book focuses on the doctor side of the doctor-patient relationship. What attracts us to medicine? What motivates us? What keeps us going? And what can "addict" us to medical practice? What do we doctors learn from our patients, from a life interwoven with health and loss of health, illness and fear of illness, death? How do we cope with daily, hourly demands from others who want us to focus on their pressing, crushing troubles?

The attraction to medicine and the enduring motivation to continue in that profession is problem-solving. Together with this detective work, awareness of medical emotions enriches us and enables us to feel that: "It is a good life".

As doctors, we interface with our patients' loaded emotive experiences. Do we realize that at the same time we are experiencing comparable although dissimilar emotions? The feelings are comparable in that fear of death and disease is universal. They are, however, dissimilar because it is not OUR disease or disability that we are confronting.

Physicians underestimate the hazards of the emotional impact of our occupation. How do the emotions of a physician find expression when we are constantly barraged by the emotional impact of our patients? Most of us just think that we have to "get on with the job". And so we do. Some very effectively and others with a mask of effectiveness.

In our life-practices, we are not only diagnosing disease, teaching health and giving practical instructions. Clearly we are also exposed to the moods and feelings of our patients who project onto us anger, grief and joy. Patients are angry and disturbed because of the situation of their illness or disability; this is independent of personal anger that they may feel towards the practitioner. Doctors give back to them moods and feelings. These medical emotions require to be acknowledged, not put into deep freeze.

The self-inflicted death of a Max jars us to remember that emotional blockade can potentially build up forces that explode into self-destruction. In addition, in order to re-energize our reserves, we have to detach and periodically to withdraw from continuous sickness situations.

If the tidal wave of daily hassles swamps us and overrides these inherent emotions, they may erupt later with volcanic, undigested, imperfect and inappropriate display. By revealing the emotions of these situations I hope to increase understanding of certain patterns of our behavior, and to relieve doctors of some of their guilt born out of unexamined or misunderstood feelings.

I write for the medical student and the young intern and resident, whose environment and natural maturation are rapidly changing their views about life and their chosen profession. Along with their own intellectual curiosity, young practitioners need emotional equipment to help prevent frustration, unrealistic expectations, and unexpected bitterness which can become a cloak for deeper emotions of fear and anxiety.

Senior doctors who are role models for younger ones in medicine do well to encourage mutual sharing of emotional involvement, sometimes turmoil or confusion, to show humility, and to increase the atmosphere of understanding and acceptance of their humaneness. When involved in a highly-charged situation, we may use conformity, and confuse strength with rigidity.

Teachers in universities and medical schools are modifying medical training in the formative years, to include courses on the psycho-physical by-products of the medical profession. In addition to the difficult task of covering a staggering number of technical facts, teachers can inspire others with the joy of persistent learning throughout life.

The study of medicine attracts young people with a sense of adventure and the lure of powerful information about human nature. Along with discovery and problem-solving, comes the satisfaction of a job well done, with conscientiousness, loyalty to patients, pleasing people, gaining respect, enjoying hard work, and being attracted to heroics with access to the knowledge of our psycho-physical fabric.

I wish to pass on the message of the attraction of discovery in medicine, and to remember the tales of patients' heroism and doctors' sharing. While aware of the potential hazards of medical practice, we can build up our reserves with which to respond to the needs of others, and enjoy diversity. The practice of medicine is changing rapidly but the stories told here illustrate human relationships which will continue to be relevant, (see Chapter 24).

Although content with my choice of a lifetime in medicine, I am deeply aware of the present problems of health care. Therefore I wish to encourage younger people to be alert to medical emotions and to seek solutions. As doctors, we accept the challenge of being hurt. Harm can be prevented, however, when we work so that the emotional needs of the medical practitioner are woven into the two-way stream of interpersonal relationships between patients and doctors, and realize that these needs are acutely related to those of the patients.

With sensitivity but without blindness, we can keep our ideals, and remain proud of saying that we have ideals. I trust that the young generation of doctors and the public understand that accepting the challenge of medicine continues to be a worth-while endeavor.

CHAPTER 2

Early Motivation

I stepped out of Waverley Station and onto Prince's Street. It was a September evening. The skyline of Edinburgh Castle and the pinnacles on the buildings on the Mound were outlined against a red sunset. Wordsworth said : "My heart leaps up when I behold a rainbow in the sky" and mine leapt up that evening because I was free to do what I wanted: to start as a medical student.

I had never set foot in Edinburgh and had no plans as to where to stay that night. I carried only a rucksack; but I held a vital passport, a little piece of paper that stated: "Present yourself at 9 AM on September 21st at the Registration Desk for Medical School". I walked out of the railway station in the sunset glow and fell in love with the skyline of the Castle on top of its rock.

That night I stayed at the YWCA, sleeping between starched sheets in a row of beds. I hated dormitories but who cares where one lives for a few days? I didn't know why I wanted to do medicine and knew very little about the subject except that I wanted knowledge. The inborn drive of curiosity and the feeling that "knowledge is power" were strong motivations, although in those days I did not think in those terms.

I had almost no experience or information about the medical profession, but had been working as a nurse for two and a half years in military hospitals during World War II. I was tired of being told: "Use a teaspoon for this medication, Nurse; and a tablespoon for that one," without understanding what I was doing. I presume (now) that I was rebellious when not knowing the ratio-nale for action, although my upbringing had given me a keen sense of duty, and I did not mind doing what I was told, being an overtly obedient child. Silent inquisitive-ness however, was strong.

Why do people want to do medicine? There are a legion of answers to that question, and it is easy to rationalize, but most decisions in life are based on emotional drive, arising from the impact of a scene. I had several scenes that motivated me towards medicine.

One December night as a nurse I was put on "special duty" to watch a young soldier who had shot himself in the chest attempting suicide. The lamp was low, the ward was quiet, the blankets grey and the sheets cold. Although he was breathing next to me, it was as though I were alone, and he were already far away, maybe going to die, going to cross the Waters of Lethe. Charon was waiting to ferry him over. What did that mean?

I had romantic ideas of death, but here was the prosaic situation that maybe he would stop breathing and I had to take action. All night I watched him as he sat propped up in bed. My duty was to take the pulse at the wrist (nothing modern like a cardiac monitor), to watch the chest and count the respirations, willing him to breathe. In the half-dark I was frightened: What do I do if the pulse stops? What do I say to him when he comes round? Will he be angry with me when he wakes up and finds himself in a military hospital and not in heaven, having been prevented from doing what he wanted to do?

In those days I thought that doctors had answers to these questions. I wanted to have answers and to be equipped with armamentarium beyond the job of recording the pulse and the respiration. I wanted to be useful. I wanted power. Poetry does not stop death; maybe knowledge and action do. If I were to obtain that knowledge, I had to climb the ladder and become a doctor.

Another formative experience was in Tidworth Military Hospital on Salisbury Plain. It was 6 AM on a May morning on a busy surgical ward. I was on night duty and two of us nurses had charge of a long ward of 20-30 beds; every patient had to be washed, given breakfast, bedpans and have their bowels and bladders attended to, wounds dressed and bed clothes tidied, before the medical officer made his rounds at 8 AM.

In addition I had my private "Rose" ritual. Whenever one of the soldier-patients had a birthday, I would slip out at dawn and steal a rose from the garden next door; (Tidworth Army Hospital stood alongside a "stately home"). When the rose was placed by the bedside of the solider with a birthday, it would be the first thing seen as he opened his eyes and the day would start with a rose.

That morning I scurried past the bed of the birthday-king in a hurry, handing out wash-bowls. He accosted me with:

"Can't you even give us a smile, Nurse? You'd look much nicer if you knew how to smile!" I was deflated like a burst balloon: had he not looked at the rose? I couldn't tell him that I had rushed out on the wet grass to pick him the rose, and that I was late with my routine duties and about to get into hot water with my superiors. The medical officer was coming and everything had to be spic and span for the great man.

The medical officer was not expected to have a smile for everyone. It was nurses, women, who were expected to be smiling on all occasions. I wanted action, not just smiles. Couldn't I find a profession in which action rather than an indefatigable smile was the most important feature? Looking back on the scene, I now see the illogicality because indeed I attached importance to the rose, which presumably was a symbol of the smile. But I wanted action, i.e. the rose to be appreciated rather than the smile. Further still, I preferred a role that involved overt action to one that required behavior which I considered at that time to be superficial.

One day a few months later, an experience gave me confidence and the taste of a skill that gave me pride. Following an air raid on the city of Bath, there was a shortage of staff for the number of emergencies. I was standing by the anesthetist when he was called away to start off treatment on a more severely injured patient. So he turned to me and said: "You know what to do Nurse. Here, take this and keep the anesthetic going". I held the mask over the patient's mouth and nose as I watched the instrument dials. I can feel to this day the rigidity with which I stood by the patient's head as he lay, anonymous on the stretcher. The surgery did not last long, but it was long enough for me to feel the thrill of responsibility. I went to bed that night with the ambition of taking charge in treatment situations.

At that time working in hospital, however, I didn't know how to proceed towards my dream. I was vague. My intention of trying for medical school was greeted with scepticism and cold water. My relatives said: "You can never be a doctor, because you're not practical enough; you're too scatter-brained. You're up in the clouds." A desire to prove the contrary probably reinforced my resolution.

At official interviews, I knew by instinct that the screening committee members were thinking: "That slip of a girl won't stick to it." Their disbelief, however, did me no harm: contrariness is a feature that gives doctors staying power, and contrariness helps one to enjoy a challenge.

Hunger for knowledge, a belief that knowledge brings power, ambition to prove oneself, endurance, and reliance on self are all characteristics of the medical profession. Fierce individuality and inner rebelliousness is particularly marked in many doctors.

Surveying this list of the characteristics of motivation at the start of a medical career, it looks similar to the motivation in very many careers of ambitious, energetic young people. It is the response to the challenge of: "Meet the World in which we live". The personal circumstances in which the individual finds him or herself probably determines the particular field to which that person puts their energies. The circumstances of World War II put me into the hospital field, and therefore harnessed my energies.

"Interest in people" and "wanting to help" is often cited by medical students as motivation for medicine. At this early stage, it may not be easy to recognize that when "interest in people" is linked with knowledge of the workings of the body (the psycho-physical person) the individual who acquires that knowledge, in this case the doctor, easily assumes a parental role of "I know what is best for you". Not only does the role bring with it a natural parental characteristic, but the recipient of the services, the patient, tends to put that responsibility onto the one whose job it is to have the necessary knowledge.

If, together with the growing sense of power that knowledge brings, the young medical students lose their imagination, the stage is set for conflict with the patient and disillusionment for the doctor.

Similar characteristics - self-reliance, fierce individuality and inner rebelliousness - motivate certain patients when they consult physicians. Just what doctors value in themselves may be present in those whom they treat.

This book is written in the hope that we can identify with the two sides of the situation - doctors and patients - and realize that they have much in common. The particular context of the relationship leads to differences.

The meeting between patient and doctor starts at a moment in time which is intensely memorable for the patient. It is often a highly-charged emotional situation for the patient, whereas for the doctor it is an event on a conveyer-belt of experiences, each of which is individualized but which occurs many times a day for many years. It requires constant use of the imagination to remember this difference in the perspectives of doctor and patient.

Changes in motivation obviously take place as a long medical career develops, partly with universal changes in age and interests. Here we are only considering the initial motivation when starting a medical career.

The particular pitfall in medical training is that imagination gets squashed under a mountain of factual details which need to be covered during years of youth and idealism. It is easy for doctors to steamroll their imagination and to repress the rose on the bed table at dawn. There is no room for giving credit to imagination.

Medical students are not aware of the anger that the patient feels against the fact of their illness. They have not had the chance to imagine the anger of the man who wakes up in a military hospital rather than in heaven. Later on, when they have qualified as doctors, that anger knocks at their door, but they have to deal with the pulse of the dying man and they do not allow the anger to enter their consciousness. It would impede their effectiveness in the acute moment requiring action.

In the daily round of telephone calls and emergency situations, how do we cope with our imagination? What do we do with the interruption that comes from the repressed unconscious? Do we tell it to "Go sit on the back burner?" One of the challenges of a medical career, which is not seen when early motivation carries the student and the young doctor through the forest of facts, is the technique of shifting our focus of attention. In the morning one is a practising doctor, in the evening maybe a young lover, and in between time one needs to swallow a telephone book of facts so as to remain on top of the action situation.

Motivation needs to be strong to carry one through the quagmire of a medical career. Maybe it is useful that most of the pitfalls are hidden and that the complexity of the situation unfolds itself only gradually throughout life.

CHAPTER 3

Can I Accept Responsibility?

Once upon a time I was a medical student. Then came the metamorphosis into a doctor. What change is required?

Every day as medical students we walked through the pathology department on our way to lunch to observe the day's autopsy. The pre-lunch hour was chosen for learning at autopsies because classes were over and the pathologist worked at that time.

As I opened the door into the autopsy room I stepped across the drain that carried the blood out of the room. The smell of the disinfectant, of formaldehyde and sometimes of the body (depending upon the cause of death), mingled with the sight of the white tiles, the washed-down slabs and the organs in the process of display. The body lay on the center table which stood like an altar, with the pathologist administering. Would the case that day be interesting? The association of being hungry at midday and of watching autopsies with the smell of the post-mortem room still to this time arises in my mind.

One day Dr. Braithwaite, the distinguished pathologist, spotted the stethoscope hanging on my shoulders over the white coat and said to me: "Is that the emblem of being qualified and on the staff?" In those days, only qualified physicians carried a stethoscope.

I was barely able to mumble an assent, because I was shy at accepting a role that carried responsibility. However I can still feel the glow of glory with which the "admission" to the profession warmed the cockles of the heart. And I understand now why nurses and many health care professionals carry stethoscopes round their necks as a badge.

That day I stood looking at the half-dissected human body Dr. Braithwaite was neatly laying out on to the stone slabs, weighing the liver, the brain, the heart and each organ carefully. This had been our patient until the night before. As Dr. Braithwaite carried the liver in his hands to put on the scales on the side table, I leaned over to look inside the abdominal cavity. My hand touched the cold white slab, and the sleeve of my white coat got stained with blood. I withdrew an inch or two, because that afternoon I was to return to examining patients and blood stains would be unpalatable.

Dr. Braithwaite meticulously demonstrated the many facts of which I and the other doctors who had treated that lady had been unaware in her lifetime. There were gallstones in the gall-bladder which had not made their presence known. The right coronary artery was blocked by atheroma, but the patient did not report heart symptoms. The liver was shiny and loaded with fat, cutting in a characteristic "slithery" way, but we had not taken alcohol into consideration. The lower lobe of the left lung was partially consolidated and there might have been an embolus. The brain weight was below normal and showed frontal lobe atrophy, but the patient's intelligence was not deemed "below par". Finally the cancer of the ovary for which the lady was under treatment had metastasized far more widely than we had imagined. The abdominal cavity was "peppered" with tumor.

At that moment of visual revelation, the weight of responsibility fell on my shoulders. It is our responsibility to obtain the facts. We had not missed the main diagnosis but there was so much more to know. Standing next to the body, I lit a Woodbine cigarette, and watched the smoke curl. I resolved to examine more closely the patients who were at that moment under my care still lying in bed, and not yet on the polished table. I felt responsible for all the people who came with their pressing complaints. Maybe they were never aware of the disorders which were really the important ones. Maybe the symptom of which they complained and which seemed important to them was only the tip of the iceberg. I felt responsible for detecting the many troubles below the surface.

I went off to lunch, just having time to grab a sandwich before the afternoon clinic was to start. Walking quickly past the line of expectant patients, seated on the benches of the Outpatients' Department, I was thinking: "How many of them are sitting there with undetected diseases! How close we are to the autopsy table, but in life how far we are from the discovery of reality! I OUGHT to know what is hidden under the skin. I OUGHT to be able to find out". Here was the "oughtism" of responsibility.

One of the junior doctor's responsibilities in our hospitals was to ask the relatives for autopsy permission. Our youthful and respectful pursuit for "truth" frequently met with rebuffs. The desperate need for answers is often not understood by the emotionally vulnerable relative. We know that autopsies reveal the correct physical diagnosis and the extent of disease. But how do we explain that the unrelated or partially related factors come to light with a post-mortem, together with the pathology which caused no obvious symptom during life, and that this is an essential part of medical practice? This process gives the doctor a surgeon's perspective, an appreciation of the spatial relationships of the body, of the architecture of the house we inhabit, of the pump, the plumbing, the walls, the chambers and the skeletal rafters. When I can see, touch, feel and smell pathological organs, I believe that I gain insight into the human scene.

The responsibility for life and the responsibility for death are part of a physician's life. Throughout medical life, this responsibility is alternatively a source of dignity, a joy, a burden, a nuisance, a trap for "infant omnipotence", a useful label or a hindrance.

The crossing of the Rubicon from the caterpillar of a medical student to the butterfly of a doctor is an irrevocable step. Nearly all other life-situations are mutable. Marriage can be ended by divorce; houses, spouses, nationalities, employment can all be changed. But once a practising physician, one cannot escape responsibility unless one specifically denies involvement. I do not include in this statement all those who study medicine but never treat patients, such as the poets Keats, Crabbe, Cowley, Robert Bridges, Francis Brett Young, the writers Rabelais, Smolett, Turgenev, the musician Kreisler and many others. Only those with commitments to patients, called "clinical" commitments, have this particular relationship of responsibility, guilt, worry and inter-personal bonding with their clientele.

Anxiety, insomnia, and a varying degree of being so wrapped up in our own medical work that we ignore personal affairs and close off other people and interests, are allied with this responsibility. We can become enmeshed in hospital events without being able to see anything else on the horizon. Among the many events that become engraved in memory, anxiety about mistakes remains prominent. I learned this at an early stage.

As young doctors we administered intravenous injections of certain drugs. I prided myself in dexterity with the needle, so that if injections had to be given at night, I did not wake the patient up.

One night at 10 PM, I went to the appointed bedside using a little flashlight, so as not to require the brighter bedside light, and I injected the medication into the vein in the arm. The patient stirred and turned over in his sleep. Back in the doctor's office, I rechecked my syringe, and found to my horror that I had given ten times the dose, having misread the decimal point of the fluid concentration. That meant that the blood would clot ten times slower than planned (in those days the methods of administering medication were less mechanically regulated). I sweated with a rising headache. Throughout the night, I went to the bedside every fifteen minutes and tested the clotting time in a micropipette, rotating the thread-like pipette between middle finger and thumb to see whether the blood was still remaining fluid. I kept thinking: "Please, blood, hurry up and clot".

The patient slept undisturbed; the blood clotted again as desired by 5 in the morning, and nobody was the worse for the mistake. While writing up the report of the incident, and devising ways to avoid the problem in the future, I realized that the personal anxiety jolted me into practical awareness of routine responsibilities. Anxiety is more effective for learning to shoulder responsibilities than guilt.

Anxiety and worry gnaw at both the patients and the physicians. The public probably has difficulty in visualizing their doctor waking up at 2 AM thinking of the many facets of a case, or pondering over a diagnosis in the bathtub. When a patient slams a doctor's door shut in evident annoyance after a consultation, I doubt that he/she wonders whether the physician feels as uncomfortable as the door slammer. Probably the patient indeed feels bad if the door were slammed intentionally, but not if it were unintentionally. Fears and resentment are often not recognized at the time or ever at all.

What do we envisage when we dream of becoming a doctor? We may think only of what we as doctors will "do for patients". We do not sit down to think of what patients will "do for doctors". Maybe we want "to help", "to save", "to pioneer", "to make discoveries". It is not easy to realize that "giving help" carries with it responsibility which can become a burden. This kind of early dreaming about one's career is not useful training for taking on responsibility, mainly because of lack of experience at that stage of dreaming. Significantly, the two-way stream of an inter-relationship is more difficult to envisage. It is hard to visualize the effort of a life-long struggle of coping with people who on the whole do not desire our services, and who, when they do call us in, really wish that the need for us would just go away.

Patients, like other people, in a civilized society do not usually say: "Go away, I don't like you!" to the individual they have just consulted. In reality they are at the same time saying "Go away" to the situation that brought them into contact with the doctor, either at an acute crisis time or in a lifelong situation. This occurs for example with multiple sclerosis, auto-immune deficiency syndrome (AIDS), a spinal cord injury causing paraplegia or a head injury with change of personality.

How do doctors learn to accept the responsibility of being the unwanted and the disliked partners in this irrevocable situation?

It is not difficult when the patient and the doctor are partners in a battle against a situation, but it is disturbing when the one who sees himself or herself as the sufferer views the other as benefiting from the situation. In that case, the doctor needs to shoulder the responsibility of experiencing the antagonism. This is the paradox of medical care. This exemplifies the old saying: "don't kill the messenger".

To be in a "responsible" position is, at first, flattering to the ego. It builds up the image of a knight on a white horse, rescuing damsels and "standing tall in the saddle". However, overloading with responsibilities that have become unwanted sours the situation. At that point the doctor's behavior can become antagonistic or self-destructive. If and when this change occurs, he or she must go and climb a high hill and overlook the entire battlefield.

How are doctors to react to the effects of continuous responsibility? To experience it as a source of interest and satisfaction rather than a burden, and a trap for dogmatism and pompous behavior? The doctors who take time to express their emotions in activities outside the practice of medicine are more able to keep their zest for learning and to adapt to the changing scene of health care.

This requires imagination and a high level of energy. It worked well for doctors such as William Carlos Williams, the poet-physician; for William Osler the Canadian physician who worked in Oxford, author of medical textbooks and philosopher-teacher, and for Oliver Wendell Holmes, author of The Autocrat at the Breakfast Table, who was active in both medicine and literature. The neurologist Henry Head published poetry in 1919, stirred by World War I. The neurophysiologist Charles Sherrington, Nobel prize winner for medicine, wrote poetry with constant awe for the wonders of the brain. Numerous others are recorded in the published anthology "Poet-Physicians".

Perhaps more important than the analysis of the achievements of a few energetic and perceptive souls is the question as to where and how do the feelings of the lonely, anxious, sensitive (perhaps "over-sensitive") doctors find outlet? Many of these find it hard to accept responsibility for both their patients and themselves.

The percentage of "impaired physicians" is extremely high. The suicide rate of doctors, particularly women doctors, is extremely high. The risk of alcohol and other drug abuse in the medical profession is higher than in the rest of the population. Women doctors appear to be less likely to abuse (according to surveys of Canadian and American treatment programs) but loneliness, inability to share responsibility and lack of a sense of achievement may be greater problems than for their male colleagues.

Why is there also such a high incidence of other stress-related disorders in doctors? Some will say that it is because of failed expectations. We, both the doctors and the public, build up unrealistic expectations of what can be achieved. Disappointment is therefore sure to follow. When doctors feel that they belong to a profession responsible for satisfying these demands, even when they involve unrealistic expectations, their personal failure rate is understandably high.

Both doctors and the public forget that the "good old days" were the days of acute rheumatic fever, of coughing up blood dying of tuberculosis, screaming with meningitis, choking with a film of diphtheria in the throat, and dying young of a heart attack. We forget that in many situations "medicine" now offers choice, the choice of remaining active long after the appointed three score years and ten. But choice involves education and the sharing of responsibility. Sharing implies a team with not only a common goal, common problems and common information, but also different skills. The responsibilities differ. And we need to understand the boundaries of responsibility.

The interpersonal relationship of doctors with patients is rarely discussed in our youthful medical training, because of the high pressure of factual information which must be absorbed. We all think that we know what responsibility entails, so why waste time on discussing it? Young doctors often say: "Give us hard data. Why dream? Why spend time on these vague frontiers, these factors that cannot be put into a one-to-ten scale? We have other more pressing matters to attend to."

However, some of these younger doctors are courageous enough to listen to their dreams, dreams of the responsibility of St. George killing the dragon; and of St. Christopher carrying the child across the stream as the child grew heavier and heavier. On waking in the morning, these dreams can be examined in a more practical light, and the nature of responsibility will be better understood.

The ability to shift our focus is a key to a balanced life. As Mary McDonough wrote of Charles Sherrington, the neurophysiologist: "If doubt remains that two minds can work at once in the same brain, the proof can be found in his writings by comparing the coincidence of his medical and poetical writings". We cannot all become poets, but all of us can learn how to evaluate, to share and to balance responsibility.

CHAPTER 4

Unavoidable Sadness

I was lying in bed. The cold Edinburgh dawn seeped through the iron bars of my one-roomed basement home. I believed the room to be magical, with bones on the mantelpiece, the femur next to the clavicle, surrounded by books and anatomical specimens in glass jars, a rectum excised with its tumor, and a skull facing the alabaster Buddha.

I wrote:

> Medicine is my love
> And my love is medicine.

It was an idyllic life. I felt that I was learning new things every day. The world was one for discovery. It was adventure, power, achievement.

The telephone rang. "Doctor, Jamie is drowsy today. He is not himself. He lies with his eyes half-closed and he doesn't want his porridge."

My heart sank. It was six days since his measles rash had erupted, since the beginning of the illness. The fever had fallen and the rash was fading; he had been a lively child a day or two ago when I watched him play by the stove in the tenement kitchen while his mother nursed the baby. Drowsiness and lethargy on the 6th day after measles rash eruption could only mean one thing: measles encephalitis. I had never seen a case, but Russell Brain's Neurology describes it as a severe complication.

In the warmth of bed, I had sudden angst. How can one prevent this viral encephalitis? Injection of convalescent serum was standard advice all right, but was it a preventative at this stage? Ill-fate was falling on the McIntyre family. Maybe Jamie would drift into coma and die (10% of such cases die). Maybe worse still, he would lose his cheerful character and become irritable, un-smiling, destructive and negativistic with epilepsy and unable to learn for the rest of his life.

The textbook page was in my mind as I made coffee and dressed warmly. I turned on the ignition key of the little Baby Austin which then sputtered up the hill. "Complete recovery occurs in 25% of the cases", I said to myself as I parked the car in the Grassmarket under the shadow of Edinburgh Castle. The McIntyres lived on the 7th floor; the spiral stone staircase always smelt of cats and coal and food scraps swept into the corners of the stairs. On the seventh floor I turned to the right and met the draughty wind as I walked along the bare stone corridor. Each floor had six flats, which all shared one outside tap of cold water. I knocked on the McIntyre's door, and Mrs. McIntyre opened and said: "Thank you for coming so quickly, Doc."

Jamie lay in the closet bed, immobile, with his two brothers clambering near him. It was three to a bed in the Edinburgh slum flats. A slight stiff neck, a low-grade fever, and a listless child. Mrs. McIntyre looked at me silently, asking questions with her eyes, sensing my anxiety. I said: "You are right. Jamie was better yesterday. I did not expect him to get drowsy at this stage. We shall have to get him to hospital to see what is going on."

The two little brothers stood at the kitchen table, watching quietly. Mrs. McIntyre put her hand on Jamie's forehead and then rubbed his fingers lying inert on the rough blanket. We made plans together. Mrs. McIntyre would wrap Jamie up in a blanket and take him by bus to hospital. I would go home and telephone to prepare the nurses. Beyond that I was powerless.

I would share my anxiety with colleagues in hospital, but I could never escape the kitchen sorrow.

Jamie remained semi-comatose for a few days. Then he seemed to recover. The nurses all loved him, with his curly hair and turned-up nose. I watched anxiously as he moved all four limbs and began to ask for food. Mrs. McIntyre was at his bedside day and night, and every morning we smiled at each other. But the child never seemed to look around inquisitively and his face was a blank. At the end of a week or two Jamie went home, wrapped in Mrs. McIntyre's blanket. He returned to the care of the pediatrician and I took a job in another city.

Fifteen years later I was walking near Edinburgh Castle, taking a break from attendance at a conference on mental retardation. At that time I was in charge of 150 mentally retarded children in a hospital near London. Although measles encephalitis had been largely eradicated, other brain-damaged children seemed to be more numerous than ever.

As I stood in the street, I saw a woman holding the hand of a teenage boy crossing the road. She seemed to be pulling him along to prevent the cars from running them over, and he was screaming in an unnatural high-pitched voice. Suddenly I was shocked to recognize the curly head and the up-turned nose. But there was no smile on the face, only an expressionless irritable resistance. When the pair reached my side of the road, I stopped to talk to Mrs. McIntyre. We spoke of the obvious change in her life. She may have known all along that the road might be long, and she knew that I cared. Jamie was not mine, but I was looking after a hundred Jamies who had failed to lift their listless heads.

James was one of the most disabled measles encephalitis children: brain development had been disrupted. This disease intrigued the pathologists at the medical conference. They worked to disentangle the causes, and to differentiate between allergic encephalitis and acute disseminated encephalo-myelitis complicating infectious diseases of childhood. How important their differentiation which could lead one day to effective therapy. Sixty-five per cent of such children were, and still are, left with residual symptoms, such as paralysis, unsteady gait, mental defect, change of personality and epilepsy. How vital for us to work to find out these facts. But Mrs. McIntyre just wanted her little son to be cheerful again and to eat his porridge. Now she and the family were left with an unlooked- for responsibility.

There are many times when doctors experience the sadness of the diagnosis at the bedside immediately, because they know that the prognosis is bad. But on the occasion in the McIntyre kitchen, I had kept my thoughts to myself: there is always the hope that the individual is one of the lucky twenty-five per cent.

When a doctor is fond of a patient, it is very helpful if the relatives are equally fond of the doctor, because it adds energy to the work required by both parties. However, despite the mutual suffering, the relative should not have to carry the extra "burden" of the physician's sorrow. Mrs. McIntyre saw my distress, especially when we talked in the street about the sad life that Jamie's change of personality had caused for her. But I did not wish to add my unhappiness to her suffering. I did not wish to transfer my sadness to her.

For many reasons patients and their relatives wish to forget their doctors and the whole experience which led to this transient relationship. Doctors are often the harbingers of harsh events, the bringers of ill tidings. Even when remedies are offered, these frequently require sacrifice of both time and money, not to mention the daily enjoyment of life for the patient and the family.

At best, in a case of illness, doctors nearly always demand change of habits. They do this either directly in words or they imply it because of the circumstances. After a significant piece of medical information has been shared, nothing will ever be the same again. Change, especially illness or death, is the most difficult thing for most people to become reconciled with. No one enjoys being jerked out of their rut. No one likes being confronted with the need to make decisions, even when another person holds out the hope of "improvement" at the end of the tunnel. The individual involved has not CHOSEN that change, and therefore there is resentment at being "unfairly" manipulated by fate, God or someone else.

Doctors cannot therefore demand to be liked or even appreciated even when they themselves show a strong empathy for the patient. We physicians must not expect it, and, knowing this, it is illogical to be upset when we do not receive the recognition that we think we deserve. We also know the reasons why these reciprocal relationships carry liabilities. And yet, and yet - - what "reason" is not based on emotion? The nobility of someone like Mrs. McIntyre builds up a human relationship that spurs us physicians on to learn about causation, to prevent disasters and to empathize in irremediable sadness. That bond, however transient, makes the world a more civilized place for us all.

What did Mrs. McIntyre teach me about the human factor in medicine? What did I learn that morning in the slums of Edinburgh? I learned that the doctor's personal involvement can soften the blow of the patient's sadness, and that decision-making relieves the anxiety felt by all parties.

I learned that I wanted to be near Mrs. McIntyre when her child was sick and might not recover: that we both felt better when we stood in pain together against the measles invader. It was my place to expect the worst and to prepare for it, doing whatever I could to prevent it. It was her place to allow me to take that responsibility while she continued to hope for the best. I also learned from other observation that if a person, whether patient or relative, can not accept fate in unavoidable circumstances but instead has to rail at it and displace anger about the situation onto the nearest object (in these cases the doctor), the bitterness is doubled.

Sharing sadness with another assumes a sense of responsibility. Responsibility for others. But how does one learn to accept responsibility for oneself, for one's own actions, particularly in sad situations? Opportunities to do so often occur in professional medical situations where decisions need to be taken.

I was a young doctor. I looked out of the hospital kitchen window at the blue sea of the Waters of Leith and wept quietly. It was 7 AM and the breakfast trays were clattering by the bedsides. I stood with my back to the ward so that no one should see those tears.

Alistair McDougall had just died, and I had not been able to save him. Alistair was a shepherd and he told me tales of his sheep, white and wooly, black-faced, high up in the hills of Scotland where he walked daily with his sheepdog till he had become breathless. When the heather started to bloom this autumn, he grew short of breath.

When his legs and abdomen swelled up, he was admitted to hospital. I sat up most the night with Alistair and tried all the gamut of injections and intravenous medications in our repertoire. As a child he had had rheumatism and the loud heart murmur of aortic stenosis is still in my head as I see him sitting up in bed. He smiled through his oxygen mask; but the swelling of the ankles never went down, the blood pressure fell, and his eyes gradually closed. His body failed to respond and I felt a failure.

The sun rose over the Waters of Leith and I thought of the sheep, baa-ing in vain up the hill, and the lambs running after their mothers and nudging fiercely at her udders.

I heard the door of the ward open and my superior, Dr. Frost, walked up briskly. I went back to meet him in the corridor.

"So what happened?," he asked, "the patient seemed to be doing alright when you telephoned."

"Yes, Sir," I replied, "he was, at first. But then he stopped responding, and became more breathless. I gave him another injection and increased the rate of oxygen flow."

I was crisp and alert and bristly, reporting on the events of that long night, with the dawn failure. Dr. Frost turned on me with an accusing look and said:

"You always think that you know best. You should make more effort. It is incompetent to let a patient die."

The head nurse joined us and was listening.

"It was a difficult case, Sir, the night staff gave me their report."

Dr. Frost ignored her and walked away. His comments hurt but I was too proud to answer. I had followed step by step every one of his instructions that night, and we had done all that the books recommended. The hill was too steep for Alistair McDougall, and we never reached the top. Alistair never blamed me; he just smiled and closed his eyes.

I learned that morning never to cry on account of the bosses' disapproval if one's conscience is clear, and not to fear their reprisal or punishment, but to sit with patients, making decisions, and watching their progress up and down the escalator of life and death.

I went back to the window where the sun was shining on the Waters of Leith; I watched the waves thin-lipped and I tried to forgive myself for my failure with Alistair. Maybe Dr. Frost was right. Maybe he could have saved Alistair. I don't know. I will always ask for help. But to point the finger at a conscientious worker is not the answer. And to blame a junior who has done her best is cowardly. I have cried with relatives after a death but Alistair had no relatives and I was learning to accept unavoidable sadness.

CHAPTER 5

The Parental Role

I had recently graduated as a doctor and started working in a general hospital. It was our team's day for admitting the acute medical cases.

Ten or eleven patients had been admitted and were "tucked" into bed, with a history and physical examination written up, a provisional diagnosis made, and treatment started.

Then at about 6 P.M. a young red-haired boy aged 18 came with his mother. Douglas was an "errand boy" at a grocery. For a week his employer had noticed that he was stumbling and staggering and had accused him of being drunk. His speech became slurred which confirmed the grocer's suspicions that he was taking alcohol.

That evening, sitting at home at supper, Douglas became dizzy and saw double. His mother, alarmed, brought him to hospital. His only previous illness had been chicken pox. He was shy and reluctant to talk about himself, scared of the hospital, unaccustomed to being examined undressed and at sea.

Unfortunately, the presumptive diagnosis was not difficult to make. It was my first personal case of multiple sclerosis, but we had seen several patients in our training. Douglas lay in bed in an awkward position, surprised that his legs were numb and wondering why he was seeing two window frames instead of one.

When his mother anxiously asked me what was wrong, what was I to say? I told her that we would be examining her son further and that he would most likely improve within a few weeks. She answered: "I trust you doctor, you will make my son well".

Yes, he did improve and returned to work at the grocery; but six months later, I saw him again with numbness around his waist like a girdle, and weakness of the left leg. Investigations confirmed the diagnosis of multiple sclerosis. I worried: Could I have prevented that girdle of numbness? Was Douglas heading towards a life of recurrent paralysis?

We treated Douglas, using the most up-to-date protocol and medication available at that time, and we asked him if he would join a research project that my professor was directing. Douglas's mother was delighted at the special attention, and Douglas went along with it. Over the next five years, we examined him at regular intervals. By then he had a girl friend and would chat about all his plans for the future.

He remained in the research group for the next 20 years, and although I moved to another city he corresponded regularly. When I visited his home town, he would arrange to bring his little son and we would enjoy his latest achievements together. I felt like a mother watching his life developing He was one of the lucky ones with multiple sclerosis who did not look back, although subtle signs of the disease persisted. He attributed his good progress to our special concern, but we had to put it down to chance because of the variability in the course of the disease. Douglas was part of our study of multiple sclerosis, but he was also part of my widespread family group.

Andrew was a tall, lanky, quiet man aged 30 when he first consulted me. He came with his wife who was deeply worried because her husband dragged his right foot and their small son said sadly:

"Daddy doesn't run anymore."

Andrew made light of his difficulty, but his wife confided to me when he went out to go to the examination room:

"Andrew feels bad because recently he has become impotent."

The diagnosis was clear: Andrew suffered from multiple sclerosis. Despite all treatment, he went steadily downhill. He lost his job as electrician in a small town, and could only walk a few stiff steps with his walker. He grew more and more silent, but would still smile when we met in the Physical Therapy Department or in the street.

For several years thereafter, he became increasingly dependent on me as he slid down the social scale with his disability. In addition to treatment that was constantly required for individual symptoms, he tacitly accepted parental support as part of doctoring. Both of us felt the need for this relationship. I was the one who had been with him under his changing circumstances over two decades. And when he died, his wife came to thank me.

Marilyn was a pretty young woman who at the age of 12 had been a prize ice-skater.

She first consulted me when aged 19 because she was suddenly unable to fasten the safety pins of her baby's diapers with her numb fingers. She was staggering all over her home, unable to climb the stairs. She and her husband were scared stiff. It was all so unexpected, and they were still adjusting to the birth of their first child. Over the next few days in hospital, she had difficulty in controlling her bladder and lost the use of her legs.

A photograph of her on the ice-rink sat by her hospital bed.

We confirmed the diagnosis of multiple sclerosis, discussed it at length and treated her. Marilyn and her husband wanted to be in command of the facts; they took a realistic and positive attitude, but Marilyn's mother, who was looking after the baby in her home, was reported to be in tears. Marilyn improved and walked out of hospital, eager to rejoin her child. "We will do whatever is necessary, Doctor," said her husband. "Yes certainly, we shall keep in touch".

Marilyn came for examination each year, keeping a faithful diary of events, and bringing photographs of her daughter growing up. Every facet of her life was looked into, with her husband participating. We discussed the risks of having another child, and fortunately their good planning was rewarded with Marilyn remaining well after the birth of a second girl.

Over the years, she only had one episode of recurrence, which we treated vigorously, and she was able to rest, to stop her baby-sitting job temporarily, and to adjust family life. At the age of 44, Marilyn reported that she had satisfied her ambition by taking up non-competitive ice-skating again. Her two daughters had graduated from college, and her husband had promotion on his newspaper. She and I rejoiced.

As doctors, we derive parental joys, watching our "family" of patients and their families grow up. We know that it is not our doing. The disease-process goes its own course in the patient's life. A doctor is always on the outside perimeter of that life. However, I and my medical colleagues satisfy our parental needs together with our professional ones.

Emergency situations require a parental role of a different kind. This is the dictatorial parent who takes charge, like an army captain.

It was an April blizzard. Snow fell late that year and we were all taken by surprise that Saturday. Lizzie took out her parent's car to go and meet her boy-friend. But in the heavy snowstorm she missed the corner of the road and struck a telephone post.

She lay unconscious on the stretcher in the emergency room. The routine was quickly followed and the team went to work. I found the airway clear, the blood pressure falling, the pupils unequal, the limbs flaccid; the X-ray was done, the cardiogram read, the blood typed, the neurosurgeon called and Lizzie taken to the operating theatre.

Two hours later, I sat with Lizzie's mother.

"Lizzie never told me she was going out. We didn't have a chance to say good-bye. Is she all right, Doctor? Will she play the piano again?"

In my momentary silence, Lizzie's mother guessed. Sometimes a doctor can share his or her grief with a mother as a vicarious parent. In emergency situations, this can only be transient. In long-term cases, the bond becomes a source of dependence.

The patients can be substitute children. A kindly doctor can act as a caring parent to those patients who like to visit and be told what to do, what to take, what to inject. For people with a chronic disorder, there is a need to pass the time of day and be refreshed by a smile, a timely piece of advice in a crisis, an encouragement on a lonely road. Someone who cares. Someone who takes notice. In this way both parties feel good. A doctor gives time and thought to patients, as does a vicarious parent.

But one day I was talking with the son of a doctor, a sullen teen-ager, who was admitted after an epileptic seizure from a bout of alcohol. I said to him:

"Did your father not warn you of the danger of alcohol?"

He turned on me and cried fiercely:

"My father is never there. He is always with the patients or away at meetings."

I had no answer.

It is easier to advise people what to do rather than to face personal problems. Even in the best of circumstances, the dilemma with a medical practice is how far to be a parent to patients, what may be termed a substitute parent, and at the same time develop the skills of a biological parent.

The idealized parent is always on call, all-loving, all-supportive, omniscient, wise, slow to anger, responsible. The good parent watches over the frail; intervenes when needed; advises but is not angered when good advice is ignored; is available for the dependent, but knows when to let go.

How do doctors slip into a parental role? How do they fit the picture of this idealized parent? Do they enjoy the role? How much are doctors prepared to forget "the child" within themselves as they adopt the ever-present parental role? How much can they synthesize the "adult" which should be themselves into this model?

I doubt that these questions were ever in our thoughts when we applied for medical school, or when we took the endless exams to qualify for the job.

Doctors may be afraid of losing status by keeping the child within themselves alive. They may fear to look weak by acknowledging their fears. They may fear to enjoy simple pleasures or humor in a professional situation. Or fear to look stupid by referring to the book to check the latest medication and its interaction with other drugs. But parents can admit mistakes without losing respect. And humility wins admiration.

Do doctors discuss this professional parental role with their potential partners when they contemplate marriage? I don't think that I and my friends ever put these matters into words until I had practised medicine for a decade or two. I was too busy doing and living. I was on a roller-coaster of experiences, day and night, happy at being "needed" apparently by one and all, and catching my personal life on the wing.

Considerations of the parental role of doctors only emerged with time and personal experience. No doubt it would be wise to have a policy of "look before you leap", but this is hard to achieve, considering the pace of life in youth.

I chose the course of a substitute parent rather than a biological one. Without the commitment to family life, I was free to have undisturbed time to be medical detective, seeking causation of disease. Fulfilling this contract the years were passed in hospital, laboratory and library, searching with colleagues but never fully finding the clues to multiple sclerosis, this mysterious disease, to vascular disease causing strokes, and to epilepsy, this intriguing symptom of many disorders. Many of my friends envied me this type of freedom, especially when they were going through personal family crises. But I could have envied them the gratification of parenting within a closer family. In certain circumstances, the two roles can be blended.

There is yet another and significant way in which doctors are parents. As doctors, like all scientists, we are the parents of the ideas and theories that we pursue and the papers that we publish concerning the nature of disease, causation, evolution, treatment, therapeutic success and failure. These ideas and publications are our children, which give us pain and glory, disappointment and satisfaction.

Parenting is inescapable in medical practice, and doctors are appreciated for their parenting skills, the women perhaps even more than the men. The challenge for doctors is to achieve a synthesis of their parental skills with the "child within" themselves, while keeping their "adult" self alive.

CHAPTER 6

Hierarchy, With or Without Support

I was training to be a neurosurgeon. Every day patients with brain tumors were being operated and I was assisting at operation, which might last 8 or 10 hours. Some came through surgery, some never recovered consciousness. Together with my colleagues, I also examined the patients on admission, wrote up the histories, interviewed the relatives, listened to questions and fears and watched the tears. In neurosurgery, doctors are confronted with death or near death in a routine way. The precious quality of life is ever present.

One night I was on duty with a 13 year-old boy Malcolm who had a brain tumor, a so-called posterior fossa tumor. This medulloblastoma was a dangerous one, because it infiltrated the "vital centers" in the brainstem and the cerebellum, the back end of the brain. At operation that day partial removal was accomplished which was as much as could be hoped for without killing the boy. But the area controlling respiration was within a few millimeters of the site of removal. He was breathing on his own, but "automatic" respiration was endangered.

I sat by the bedside, in between all the tubes connected to intravenous and drainage procedures. In the semi-darkness under the low lamp, Malcolm breathed once in a while. Would the bedclothes rise with the next breath? Could I will him to breathe? Would 13 breaths per minute maintain life? What was I to do if the rate fell down to below the magic number 13? I telephoned my superior. The sleepy voice of the surgeon Arnold Thorne cheerfully reassured me that he expected only 13 breaths per minute, and not to worry, but to call again if I became concerned. He always had a kind way of sharing responsibility with me who was less experienced.

I returned to Malcolm's bedside, reassured, for another hour or so. Still no improvement, and the breathing got shallower.

If I were the mother, what would I feel? What would I say to her if her child should die? What would she feel towards me? I called Arnold Thorne again. The same sleepy but comforting voice reassured me. He again said: "Call if you get worried."

The dawn came. The child lived. The next emergency was to be admitted at 7 AM, and I had to leave the bedside and go and listen to another story of headache and paralysis, seizures and fear.

Over the next fifteen years, I read the articles written by Arnold Thorne in neurosurgical journals, with particular interest because I had worked under him.

One day in a hotel lobby at the annual meeting of a neurological society, I ran across a surgeon friend and asked:

"What news of Arnold Thorne?".

"Oh, haven't you heard?" came the answer, "he committed suicide last year".

I was stunned; Arnold was such a "stable" surgeon.

"Why?" I asked.

"God knows", the man replied and disappeared up the elevator.

I had never thought that Arnold Thorne had special problems. He always looked secure in his role of authority. He never really shared personal feelings but as a leader

I did not expect it. In our day-to-day hospital relationship there did not seem to be time to open up a wider view of what we were all doing.

How do we get a more general view of our colleagues' personalities, a more imaginative understanding of their emotions, a clearer vision of the hierarchical role, when the telephone rings and we make a quick decision as to which patient with a brain tumor needs urgent admission?

Hierarchy is defined as: "a body of persons organized according to rank, capacity or authority." It enters into all work situations except self-employment. In hospital medicine, both the observance and the results of hierarchy involve visible and sensitive areas. "Capacity" in hospital practice is linked with experience. In a well-functioning hierarchy with strong loyalty, competitiveness is not an issue, although individuals trying to make a mark can introduce it.

The general spirit within a hierarchy radiates from the role models in authority positions, and permeates decision-making on a daily basis.

The relationship and work-pattern within a medical hierarchy is often colored by experiences in medical school. Examples of respect and loyalty breed similar patterns of behavior. The relationship of the medical student to the professor, however, is one of example. Once the student becomes a doctor, responsibility is shared out, and honesty and conscientiousness become all-important.

In the early professional years, hierarchy chiefly implies the degree of responsibility and the availability of a superior in decision-making. That individual is older and deemed superior in experience. Whether he/ she is also superior in expertise depends upon the task in question; generally speaking, the more experienced is superior in judgement and overall knowledge, but often not in specialized information and in technique. Because change in medicine is even more rapid than in other fields, the frustration of juniors gets mixed up with personal ambition and youthful reluctance to listen to others.

What doctors learn from each other varies greatly over the world. We are particularly vulnerable to the atmosphere and climate of the working situation, because the patients and all those looking after patients are emotionally charged. Our behavior is contagious. Our loyalties are built-in early. We would profit from sharing within the hierarchical system the personal joys and sadnesses derived from our work. Generously shared experiences solve problems, both personal and professional.

Doctors learn from each other by observation. We see each other stepping into the elevator with serious faces at 7.30 AM in order to show up keenly at the breakfast meeting; we watch colleagues in emergency rooms, in the operating room, and at the bedside of the dying; talking with nurses, doing procedures, meeting relatives. Years of observation are spent sitting at the back of the lecture room listening to a hundred papers read at medical meetings. Relaxing in the common room, stories are exchanged, and laughter, appropriate or inappropriate, often relieves tension. We recount drama and surgical techniques; or the worries of people who come with "unbearable" tinglings which, although alarming to the patient, are of no medical consequence. We meet colleagues up and down the hospital corridors at 2 AM, tired, worried or in a hurry to get back to bed.

The conversations in the common room, the operating theatre changing rooms, and in the hotel foyer at medical conferences reveal mood, attitude and behavior patterns. The new man or woman on the block appears perpetually busy and displays a prominent beeper. The white coat is worn or left off according to projection of image of efficiency, or because of insecurity or status, or copying the style of one's "chief", or merely habit. Individual cases are minutely discussed from the medical, technical point of view, but the personal side of our involvement is rarely brought up. In that context it is considered irrelevant. Professional experiences are not easily fitted into private life. Despite the difficulty, for example, of dove-tailing the work in a hierarchy with falling in love, there is a need to balance personal with professional loyalties because these both influence medical decisions. "Balance" often requires compromise.

In emergency situations, there cannot be compromise, and personal life takes second place to clinical medicine. When the hierarchy is well-defined and strictly adhered to, efficiency is maximized. In non-emergency cases, we can sit down and discuss our behavior and how it affects others.

How do we learn the "correct" or more kindly expressed, the "appropriate" use of time?

The neurologist, Dr. Russell Fraser, advised me one day as the telephone rang in the doctors' room at our hospital near Oxford:

"Let the secretary answer first, don't waste your life on the telephone".

He was courtesy itself, and always answered everyone as if he had a clear understanding of their problem and gave them his undivided attention. The patients, however, never realized that he might be answering their questions without remembering the particulars of their situation. It requires great skill to carry on a conversation appropriately while following independent train of thought at the same time. Dr. Fraser, being Professor and Chairman of the Department, spent most of his time planning and relating to the world outside the hospital and the department. Because he delegated well, we understood his lack of awareness of the details of our problems. All we wanted was to know that if we needed his time, he would give it. In this respect, we were just like the patients.

As a doctor, to be too easily "caught" and manipulated into long conversations when one quick decision is more effective, leads to poor working habits. On the other hand, to brush off questions as if they were unimportant, (even if they may be of no importance to the answerer) is lacking in imagination. On this point, older physicians if they have listening skills can help their juniors as a model.

Behavior is influenced by our self-worth in relation to others. How much do we "need to be needed?"

Doctors, politicians and parents all need to be needed. But when they are constantly in demand, day and night, they begin to complain about "never having time to myself."

The build-up of a doctors' resistance to this role of being "always in demand" can be noted in hospital. The telephone operator is busy calling Dr. Brown, a young doctor, over the loud-speaker. At first, Dr. Brown enjoys the attention. Subconsciously there is satisfaction in gaining recognition and fame. With the calling, the staff and patients hear the name of Dr. Brown, this rising celebrity. "I am needed" is a comforting thought.

Dr. Brown newly arrived on the scene answers the telephone promptly. When, however, he is snowed under, and the prospect of yet another patient admission arises at 6 P.M. with the end of a day's work in sight, then the eagerness to answer the phone cools.

I gauged the mood of some doctors by the delay in answering telephone calls. Whenever I heard: "Dr. Roberts, please call the operator" echoing over and over again down the hospital corridor, I could guess George's mood; it often signaled yet another crisis on the home front. A storm was gathering around Betty in the kitchen with the kids. Would George spend more time on the last patient, or face the turmoil at home?

The working patterns of a doctor or other professional can usually be surmised by the tone of voice of the personal secretary. If there is a barrage of stiff, putting-off answers, a protector for "the great man", there may be a self-important personage behind the barrage. The public image of a constantly busy physician reflects a certain truth, but it is also a well-recognized and useful ploy, known to parents, lawyers, teachers and all figures implying authority.

In a hierarchy, physicians and surgeons rarely give time to the problems of their juniors. Although some are indeed "father" figures for the younger members, an adult-to-adult relationship would be productive for all concerned.

Many young doctors yearn for the opportunity of meeting their seniors in a private setting, best of all in the home. The summer Department picnic in a public park in no way fulfills that desire, and even less if the spouses sit watching the doctors play baseball or cricket without being part of the game. We understand that time spent with others is taken away from our personal pursuits, and that home meetings take effort and are more difficult than group sessions. However, contact outside the work environment is rewarding, and throughout history loyalty and inspiration have arisen through personal meeting.

Role models can influence us emotionally.

Dr. Ernst Levin was an eminent but humble neurologist, trained in Hamburg. He was burly and spoke with a heavy accent and I rarely heard him laugh, but he was endlessly patient and kind. He marked the records of his patients who had epileptic seizures: "Morbus Sacer", the sacred disease, because the Romans thought that people with seizures were touched by the hand of the gods. He taught us the minutiae of clinical examination and neurological rationale. After his outpatient sessions, spending more than an hour with each patient, we would drink coffee in a little restaurant, and he would tell stories.

"One day Babinski and Oppenheim (two famous neurologists) stood side by side examining a patient. They then argued about the obscure diagnosis. Oppenheim, a German, declared: "It cannot be, it is illogical." Babinski, a Russian, answered: "But, my dear friend, it IS.""

Dr. Levin used to invite me to dinner in his home. When he opened the front door, a smell of cabbage always greeted me, and Mrs. Levin would emerge from the kitchen holding a tea towel with a smile. Some years later, Ernst Levin died. I could only be thankful that he had not deteriorated with old age, and I remain deeply grateful for his inspiration.

How do we approach personal relationships and our own feelings in a hierarchy? Some people may have alexithymia, a condition in which they have no words with which to explain their emotions, or inability to express their feelings in words. Doctors may have this difficulty because of being daily bombarded with the emotions of others. They prefer, therefore, to "switch off" and play tennis or golf, to go fishing or let off pent-up feelings in physical exercise, listen to music or tell ribald stories. Emotional issues may not be discussed within the hierarchy because they are all too near the bone. However, many professionals understand that beneficial support can be built up within a hierarchy, and that this support is always remembered.

CHAPTER 7

Anxiety is a Useful Quality

When working in neurosurgery, I had a recurrent dream of doing a lumbar puncture (spinal tap) with the patient dying on me while the needle was sticking in the back. I was unable to see the patient's face, I only saw the skin on the back. The patient lay on his side curled up so that I stared at the bare back and the face was away from me. I would wake up in a sweat, just as the needle went into the patient's body and the cerebro-spinal fluid came out through the needle. With the needle in the back, the body would go limp on me and my heart-beat would stop. The cold dawn of grey Edinburgh would greet me, and the cherry tree peeping through the metal bars of the basement where I slept would reassure me. This recurrent nightmare usually took two or three nights to wear off.

Anxiety and time pressure make for a "good doctor". Anxiety pushes one to consult specialists, to look up the reference books, ask questions, grub around, wake up early to see how that patient admitted to hospital last night is faring. The recently graduated doctor has anxiety. If he/she does not, there is something wrong! He/she answers telephone calls promptly. He/she wakes at 2 AM to think over the diagnosis of a new patient. Whenever driving the car, differential diagnoses are reviewed.

My neurosurgeon chief, Alexander Brown, described to me his mental process of reviewing in his mind all the possible diagnoses of his patients whenever he was driving to-and-from the hospital. At that time I was young and naive and thought that he always knew the correct answer. I admired Dr. Brown for that brief remark showing his worry as well as his concern. The anxiety made him seem like one of us.

It was summer time, and the lilacs filled the garden with perfume. There was dew on the grass by the brick path of the Garden Cottage outside Oxford. The wisteria was beginning to bloom by the door. But my mouth was dry and my heart beat fast, and I wanted one thing only, to get to see that child with poliomyelitis to find out what was happening. The nurse had called to say that the blood pressure was rising and the respirations were more shallow. It was last night's admission and the child's restlessness had given me that feeling of unease.

When I got to the bedside, it was worse than I had feared, because Jimmie was refusing orange juice, and I could see that he knew what he was doing. He somehow realized that his swallowing had become impaired and that he might choke. So he just lay there, with big eyes, alert, apprehensive, refusing drink. In a second I realized that this was the most dangerous type of polio-encephalitis, with developing paralysis of the muscles of respiration and the "bulbar" muscles that control swallowing. Soon he might have difficulty in swallowing his own saliva.

We were between the devil and the deep sea. Jimmie was breathing irregularly and unwilling to talk, and the few words that he spoke were pronounced with a nasal tone of voice. Quick action was required. First we explained to him that changing his position would help and so we turned him prone with the head on one side. He was a very intelligent and co-operative child. Each new measure was explained and rapidly performed, but the positive-pressure respiration pump of those times was a tricky machine, and I had mounting anxiety during those long hours. Between action and watchfulness, one could but pray.

On the next Saturday I developed aching in the muscles of my legs. I was on duty and lay down in the room next to the hospital ward. I thought: "I'll just keep an eye on this." I had slight fever, and the suspicion of a headache; so I put my head on my chest to monitor possible neck stiffness. I was afraid of paralysis and the consequences. I wrote to a doctor friend giving "instructions" if the situation should change. The aching pain in the muscles increased, with slight stiffness, but no one noticed as I walked a little slower in hospital. On the third day my legs felt better and after a week or so, it was all over. The anxiety had gone and I was nicely immune to the polio virus.

Jimmie with paralysis of breathing and swallowing was gradually recovering, and we could meet his parents with a more genuine smile. But many others were paralyzed in their arms or legs or respiratory muscles and the long journeys of acceptance, hope, vigilance, realism and non-stop rehabilitation continued.

Anxiety needed to be shared with the families. Decisions which were made for the future could lighten some of those problems. Knowing where one wants to go, and planning how to get there is a great balm in times of stress.

Throughout that long summer, with the polio epidemic, I dreaded the telephone ring which might be bringing bad news. Clinical situations were constantly changing within hours, and at no time did I feel "safe". Only the closest communication with the nursing staff gave me any feeling of confidence so that I could sleep or smell the flowers in the garden.

However, the lessons of that summer with anxiety were valuable for life, being applicable to every other disease presenting with acute illness and leading to long-term disability, such as spinal cord injury or Guillain-Barre polyneuropathy. Medical alertness born out of anxiety brings determination and quick action.

What is the price to pay for this anxiety? When the conditions of seriously ill patients are in constant flux, a doctor's anxiety tends to spill over into personal life. How do these commitments to patients and professional life fit in and mesh with family life and ties? They are rivals for the energies, interest and attention of the doctor.

I knew a chemist, Rachel, who shared a house with a young woman doctor, Susan. Everyday that doctor came home with the frown of anxiety written all over her forehead.

Before Rachel could say: "What are we going to have for supper?", Susan would pour out the worries of the day: how this anesthetic had unexpectedly caused vomiting, how that patient's headache was due to meningitis and not to quarreling with the boss, how this man aged 40 had fallen off the roof and was paralyzed for life so that she, the doctor, must go back to hospital in half an hour to meet his wife, and therefore supper must be on the table in a minute.

Rachel continued to listen sympathetically to all these anxieties for three months, but after that, Rachel (who had professional worries of her own) moved out to share a house with a less anxious friend.

Can we learn to switch off from our professional worries and attend to other people's concerns?

One January, a busy doctor friend, head of a Department, told me about the trouble he had in going to buy the family Christmas tree.

Every morning at the front door, his wife would say: "Now don't forget George, to buy the Christmas tree; the tree farm is just round the corner from the hospital."

Every day this errand got crowded out with hospital commitments and his anxiety that his young colleagues were not doing their job properly with his patients. Finally, on Christmas Eve, George bought the wretched tree. But when he arrived home panting with it in his arms, there was no joy because it was too late to have time with the decorations and all the children complained.

Do spouses have cause for complaint when the anxiety and distraction intrudes into home behavior?

The supper is not cooked, the children are locked out of the house by mistake, the parent-teacher meeting is forgotten and the holiday plans are not made soon enough so that all the vacation spots are booked.

Another question arises concerning the state of anxiety. Can we combine anxiety with doing a good job? Particularly when the feeling is closely linked with personal involvement, does it interfere with efficiency? Misplaced or neurotic worrying impedes clear thinking.

Knowledge can take the edge off anxiety. One should be able to see the wood for the trees. When experienced skills develop, a doctor is able to cope with more details simultaneously and to perceive the picture as a whole.

Also at certain stages in a medical career, one may need to reduce the level of anxiety in order to protect one's sanity. The feeling that one's work is never finished is a danger. This, however, is a universal feeling amongst all dedicated professionals, and we do not need to be dissatisfied with our performance en route.

Creative tension is not the same as the anxiety discussed above.

An ophthalmologist friend often said to me that a good doctor needs to be obsessive-compulsive, so that he/she checks the details for accuracy. Working throughout a life-time with the delicate mechanism of the eye, an ophthalmologist is expected to be technically skilled like a reliable machine.

In these circumstances, the patient demands a skilled machine. And as much as humanly possible, the machine is to be fool-proof. This is the situation when well-trained doctors work with the unconscious patient, in the operating theatre, or in the dark radiology room, or the unseen laboratory, or in the recesses of the bowel, the vagina, the lung or the heart. In these cases, the patient is only sometimes privy to the scene, looking at the screen or down the tube or the microscope.

The patient is not interested in an imaginative chatty charmer; he or she wants a steady hand experienced with the probe and the dissecting microscope of technical medicine. In this situation, the automaton should be omniscient and faultless. The introspective neurotic is not appreciated.

Performance anxiety is a complex issue, and I am not describing the routine activities, in particular the manual ones, which should not cause anxiety. Technical anxieties should drop off as the doctor gets older.

It is the new and unknown situation which induces anxiety with fear. That situation may be new because the doctor is young and inexperienced. It is unknown because it involves the personality of the patient. The disease process may be well-known to the doctor. But the REACTION to that process, which is the result of the patient's personality, is not known. Therefore, meeting new patients is the cause of fatigue by the end of a day.

Anxiety in the face of new relationships should persist throughout a medical career. The associated fear is reduced when it is combined with two other ingredients. One is humility; as doctors we are treading in another person's territory in which they have more information than we do. We know about the standard disease. They know about their own feelings. The other ingredient is intellectual curiosity. There is always something new to be learned.

The practice of medicine is enhanced by anxiety, but this should be in appropriate situations and in controllable amounts. When anxiety breeds empathy, we recognize its valuable quality. When anxiety paralyses action, we criticize the weakling who is unable to make quick decisions.

CHAPTER 8

Satisfaction in Making the Correct Diagnosis

One time I was called out of the evening surgery.

"Doctor, my son fell at work today, and he is in bad pain. Will you come right away?".

I left the waiting room full of patients, saying to my colleagues that I would be back as soon as I could.

I worried as I climbed the spiral stairs to the fifth floor of an Edinburgh slum. I had never met any of the family, and I hoped that I was knocking on the right door. An anxious woman greeted me.

"Thank you for coming, Doctor. Angus is over there on the bed."

In the half dark of a room that served many purposes, the young man lay on his bed in acute pain. The pain seemed to be "all over" the abdomen and he was tender to the touch "all over", rigid and afraid to move. The pulse was rapid. It was too dim for me to see his face but it was not necessary.

Angus recounted:

"This morning I was working on scaffolding in the Grassmarket and I fell between the boards. I remained suspended in mid-air, caught between the boards. My workmates came to the rescue. I carried on with work on the ground, but the pain got so bad that I gave up. I just crawled home to lie down."

One did not need to be an experienced Sherlock Holmes to detect the diagnosis of a ruptured spleen, but for me it was exciting because it was the first that I had come across, and immediate action was required. There was no telephone in the house, but we arranged that a neighbor would drive Angus to the hospital where I worked.

Meantime I returned to our medical office and alerted the Emergency room surgeon on duty that a patient with a probably ruptured spleen was on his way to hospital.

I carried on examining the next patient, and the next. The waiting room was just emptying with the last patient going out of the door. I was beginning to put away the files when the telephone rang.

"You were right," the young surgeon said; "it was a ruptured spleen and the man might have died. I had to take the spleen out. The operation went smoothly, and Angus is doing well. Thanks for the referral."

There was a ring of satisfaction in the surgeon's voice. And as I put the phone down, I also felt a glow of satisfaction that my day's work was good and that life was really worth-while.

The most time-honored job of the doctor is to make the correct diagnosis. Medical training is directed towards this end. This is the skill which makes for the physician's main responsibility, and the basis of the art of medicine. In all cultures this is the reason for consulting the witch-doctor, or family physician, or super-specialist or the oracle at the top of the mountain. I am therefore disturbed when I cannot reach a diagnosis, and elated when it turns out to be correct.

Everyone, including a young doctor, enjoys experiences that reinforce the idea that he or she made the "right" decision in a problem situation and consequently did the "right" thing. Achievement in problem-solving is the highest satisfier in human endeavors, according to the psychologist Abraham Maslow, and illustrated by the studies in the work-place of Frederick Herzberg, author of *Work and the Nature of Man.*

I particularly needed that satisfier in those early professional days, because I had recently worked in a specialist neurological hospital in London, where it seemed to me that only the opinions of tall, well-dressed, preferably bald, males were worthy of attention. This misconception on my part needed to be modified, and change came with the responsibility of decision-making in daily medical practice.

Early in my career, I thought that medical care was simple and straight-forward: I was to make a diagnosis and take appropriate action, and it was either the "right" diagnosis or it wasn't.

However, along with medical experiences, I came to realize that in most circumstances making the "right" diagnosis, and therefore getting personal satisfaction, is a far more complicated process than with the two patients just described. Physicians learn the complexity, but it is often difficult for the patient to appreciate the many factors involved.

First, the lesion has to be identified. In this context the lesion is the demonstrable cause most closely related to the main symptom, meaning the most significant symptom and sign of disease which the patient presents.

The "most significant" symptom or sign of disease, however, may not be the one which the patient brings to the doctor. In fact very often it is not. The patient may not talk about the symptom related to what is in fact the lesion.

The doctor right away may be interested in something which does not "interest" the patient, because to the doctor this something may be the most significant factor from the medical point of view.

In many cases no one lesion is demonstrable. In other cases there is wide divergence in the nature of the lesions from the beginning.

Mark consulted me about a headache and I diagnosed muscle tension as the cause of his headache. However, in addition I detected a congenital kidney abnormality, with normal kidney function. But for Mark, the kidney was not interesting since it was not causing any present trouble and he would have preferred not to have known about it, particularly as the knowledge increased his tension headache.

I was satisfied from the medical point of view in making the correct diagnosis of kidney abnormality which Mark was born with, but not satisfied about our interpersonal relationships because Mark disliked me for telling him about it.

The "right" diagnosis for that moment would probably have been simply tension headache. Years later, however, Mark might have accused me of not making a complete and therefore "correct" diagnosis.

The lesion may clearly be the cause of the disease or disability, but it still needs to be seen in the context of the individual affected. The same type of lesion can easily affect people very differently. Hippocrates said: "I would rather know what sort of person has a disease than what sort of disease a person has." Obviously we need to know both.

Janet, aged 26, was an avid and cheerful skier who broke her leg on the ski slope. She required surgery for her fractured tibia, but then worked hard at her rehabilitation and was back on the ski runs next season. She accepted her fall since it had occurred in the pursuit of pleasure.

Dennis, aged 27, was a disgruntled factory worker who suffered a rather similar fracture of his tibia, but in an industrial accident. He had previously been injured, and he felt that he was a victim. Some months later, I treated him in the pain clinic, with the diagnosis of "post-traumatic stress syndrome, associated with fracture of the tibia", leading to a Workman's Compensation court case lasting several years.

Satisfaction depends in part on the doctor-patient relationship.

The physician might have a different attitude towards a patient whose headache is due to a brain tumor from one due to trouble with the boss. However, if this difference in the doctor's attitude were regarded as lack of interest in the headache (as opposed to concern for the boss-problem), it could seem unreasonable and in fact detestable to the sufferer of the acute headache.

"I need pills, Doctor. You are not paying attention to my needs as a person", an outraged patient once said to me.

I kept silent, but I had wanted to say: "I am trained to make the correct diagnosis. Didn't you come to me to get the truth?"

The patient had exclaimed: "All I want is to feel comfortable, Doctor," walking off looking very uncomfortable. I imagined him saying to himself: "That doctor is paid to keep me well."

There was no satisfaction in that encounter, and all that afternoon I too felt uncomfortable.

Patients are often more interested in treatment ("and please do it quickly, Doctor") than in diagnosis.

For these people if the symptom goes away, then all must be well. From the doctor's point of view, although they may be right, it depends upon the cause of the symptom. In fact it depends, once again, upon the diagnosis. My satisfaction as a doctor is to make the correct diagnosis; the patient's satisfaction is to get immediate relief.

Other patients are more interested in diagnosis than in treatment because the underlying reason for their consultation was indeed to find out the cause of the symptom. If and when the fear of significant illness is removed, then the patients wish to be independent of the doctor and to go away and forget about it all.

The physician's satisfaction in making the "correct" diagnosis is tempered by the use to which this "correct" diagnosis is put, and that depends upon how the patient reacts to this diagnosis.

Satisfaction in Making the Correct Diagnosis

In cases such as a ruptured spleen or an acute appendicitis requiring removal of the inflamed appendix, how clear are the rewards! How uncomplicated are the decisions and the emotions! How fulfilled are the textbook promises! But for most physicians, how rare are these occasions!

Most situations are more complicated, arising out of long-established patterns of behavior; and a symptom is often only the tip of the iceberg.

Every condition in the spectrum of health or disease presents both psychological and physiological aspects. In other words, a human being, at any given time, is sitting somewhere along the scale of a psycho-physiological state. (Physiology is the biological science that describes all the vital functions of an organism). When an event like a broken leg hits us, the reaction varies according to our present psycho-physiological state.

We cannot have appendicitis without reacting to it with emotion, even if transient. We cannot be depressed or cheerful without that emotion causing a physical change. The human being is a psycho-physiological whole.

Wunderlich and others denounced the concept of specific entities in disease, and urged that "pathologic physiology" be the true basis of medical science (Feinstein, 1967). In their terminology, "pathologic physiology" is used to include both the abnormal and the normal workings of the individual. In this way of viewing medicine, the "correct" diagnosis would be described differently, and doctor satisfaction might be linked more closely to health as well as disease.

Emotions of a Physician

Constant revision is required in medical thinking. The neurologist Charcot, much more than a hundred years ago, in 1857, wrote that: "Disease is very old, and nothing about it has changed. It is we who change as we learn to recognize what was formerly imperceptible".

The philosophy underlying the complex subject of making a "correct" diagnosis is of fundamental importance. The diagnosis often requires subtle modification. However, the family physician and the specialist are working with the patient sitting beside him or her. They have to satisfy and communicate with the individual and the relatives on an immediate basis.

The diagnosis has to be written on a host of medical forms. In complicated cases, doctors may be tempted just to put down the patient's symptoms. However, sooner or later in all cases somebody has to commit themselves to a working diagnosis, keeping a flexible mind open to revision at a later date.

Are the doctors satisfying themselves, their own consciences, or are they deriving satisfaction from making the patient as happy as the circumstances allow? Clearly when the two factors coincide, when both doctor and patient are satisfied, that is the ideal.

It is wise for both patient and doctor to be realistic in their expectations. In order for all parties to be satisfied, we should understand that it is always a question of making the best of a situation. That often means the best of a "bad" or at least a sad job. How are we to be "satisfied" when the result of hard work is a dead body?

How beautiful when we acknowledge that diagnosis leads to treatment which may involve choosing the lesser of two evils, and making the best of a bad bargain!

A young man, David, was a city journalist with a love of travel and adventure. While reporting in a civil war on the other side of the world, he suffered a gunshot wound causing a spinal cord injury which put him in a wheelchair for life. Was he to return to his previous newspaper and continue daily hassle on the highway to work, or take a less glamorous job on his local newspaper in the country?

One day at Eastertime I visited David who sat by the window of his home. He said to me:

"You see that yellow bird? It returns each Spring. I am paralyzed and I can't get out any more and hike in the woods. But I enjoy watching the birds fly past the window as I sit by the typewriter. I have not forgotten my injury, but I am content with a change in occupation."

Satisfaction comes from making the correct diagnosis. There will be additional bonus if that diagnosis leads wisely to a life that both patient and doctor find acceptable.

❧ ❧ ❧

CHAPTER 9

Sublimation. Can I Learn to Modify?

I was lying in bed at a friend's house on a Sunday morning. I was awakened by little footsteps in the room next door and excited whispers: "Can I go in and see her, Mum?"

Soon there came a tap on the door and two small children peeped round the corner: "Can we come in ?"

"Certainly," I answered sleepily.

They jumped up onto the bed, and pretty soon they made themselves comfortable under the bedclothes, chattering away about their Christmas presents, and rolling their toy trucks over the hills and valleys of the bedclothes.

I thought: "This is what I give up. This is what I never have." I resisted the warm snuggling of their wiggly bodies, thinking that it would make even more acute the envy I had of my friend's welcoming household, of their chattering children, of the sharing of daily experiences and of the feel of flesh, the embraces of young children.

I knew that morning that I would get up, that I would smile and thank them for the brief sharing of Sunday family life, and that I would feel better once I had managed to pull myself together, get dressed and off to the University hospital to see how my patients were doing.

Yes, it did feel better once I was back into the groove and walked into hospital and saw the smiles of patients who had slept well and were recovering . This after all was the path I had chosen, and one can't be in two places at once. My friend could practice in her Family Planning Clinic with regular hours and be a mother at the same time. But it was not possible for me to give time and emotional energy to the demands of children of my own and to patients in parallel time. The bond of affection had to be on a somewhat more distant level. The spider's web of emotional satisfaction had to be threaded onto a more distant tree. My vista had to be longer, my inner resources had to substitute for more immediate physical and emotional reinforcement in daily life.

To sublimate, (from the psychological point of view) is "to modify the natural expression of an instinctual impulse in a socially acceptable manner". This is the definition in the American Heritage dictionary. Sublimation being "the act or process of sublimating" is an art which each individual learns for him/ or herself. What works for one person may not work for another; but in every case the individual needs to have a great variety of techniques to satisfy deep desires, available for use in different situations. One sublimating activity, for example, may serve for wet winter evenings, and another for sultry summer nights.

A colleague and I often discussed the question of the satisfactions we obtain with professional activities versus those with home life.

In the laboratory this researcher and I were studying the behavior of cats, with their electro-physiological responses and their brain waves associated with epilepsy.

"Good morning," we would say to each other, "how are all the cats today?"

Walking around to look at the cats, just as one would walk round to see the hospital patients, we had our "clinic of the cats". We would observe closely our latest black marvel to see how well he was arching his back, purring and coming to rub up against our legs, and check whether he had finished eating his special dish of food.

As we sat hour after hour on summer evenings recording levels of "hyperactivity", with epileptic responses to flashing light and electro-encephalographic phenomena in the depths of the brain never previously recorded, we talked of my friend's dilemma.

He loved a woman and she wanted to marry him. But he said: "If I were married to her, I would have to go back for supper right now; we could not continue this experiment. We would never learn how that part of the brain, the ventro-medial nucleus of the thalamus, responds. I would be tied down by domestic obligations; and she understands that."

Yes, she understood it, just as I understood it.

You can't go home for supper just when discovery is round the corner and you have been hoping for this for months. Equally you can't keep somebody waiting for hours, expecting them to share your enthusiasm when they are not part of the show. Both he and I were responsible people, loving children and enjoying domestic felicities; but we had to substitute those felicitous experiences of our friends (who kindly allowed us to share a little of them,) for our own personal ones. We had to substitute exploration with cats and monkeys for exploring the world with our own kids.

If you choose the path of aloneness, you have to develop a menu of other satisfactions, a repertoire of sublimating activities. The art of sublimation is unlikely to find a place in the crowded curriculum of medical school, but the skill can be learned from examples which are abundantly available.

I asked a patient, Harry, aged 72, a retired farmer in a Midwest State mental hospital to give me a proverb. He answered:

"Laugh and the world laughs with you; weep and you weep alone." It was the first time that I had heard that saying and I thought:

"How sad! How harsh is the world he sees!" But that evening, sitting alone by a cozy wood fire, I decided that he was right. I decided that in future I would treat every invitation that came my way as a plus and make no minus note of lack of invitation.

When you come home alone and the house is dark and the curtains are not drawn, do something quickly: an open fire is company; a library is a friend for life; a musical instrument can be deeply satisfying; a well-placed telephone conversation is refreshing. Many physical pleasures, such as ski-ing or climbing mountains, are sublimation for the deeper but often tumultuously upsetting sexual adventures.

If on the other hand we choose the path of home partnership, there are other considerations. How much of the daily experiences in medical practice are we going to share with our partner? A partner does not have our same enthusiasm and cannot take on our worries. So a person can be just as "alone" whether single or partnered if there is no sharing.

One day I telephoned a friend of 25 years. "How are you both?" I asked, "we haven't seen you recently."

"Bill and I are separated." I was speechless. Not so long ago we had talked of their forthcoming celebration of 40 years of marriage. Bill had climbed the tree of medical success and Daphne always appeared at his side, ornamenting all social occasions. I was in the dark and could only conjecture.

With the daily revelations from patients in distress and the conflicting feelings which these engender, doctors may develop a wall of internal resistance to sharing. If we repress our emotions and shut the partner out of our thoughts, satisfactions, crises and our humorous situations, we may, once the children have left the nest, grow far apart. At the time of a silver or golden wedding, we may be too bored to stay together. The railway lines can only be kept open by a certain sharing throughout a career.

A repertoire of activities for his or her personal sublimation can make the path of aloneness acceptable, and the medical profession offers many such avenues.

If it were not for the warmth emanating from the satisfaction of sharing experiences with patients, the bleakness of daily medical duties would often be overwhelming. Doctors take the sadness of human suffering out of most of their days by gaining the impression that they are somehow diminishing it. Often this is an illusion. But are not illusions the source of energy in human affairs? We can at least have the illusion of doing something useful by listening.

I was sitting drinking coffee at a prestigious institution in the Midwest one snowy morning, chatting with the young physicians who were training as specialists. We talked of their hopes and plans, and one of them said:

"I would not want my wife to be spending her time with patients every evening instead of bathing the children."

I was disappointed in hearing his viewpoint. But I was glad of the fact that they were honest; and also that for them I was apparently in the category of a nun with whom they could discuss these matters, since I was clearly out of the running! There is satisfaction in being cast in the role of a listener, even of a mother-confessor: it builds up a varied and composite picture of the world, even if skewed and painful.

The technique of sublimation is not always able to satisfy personal needs. It is nobody's job to look after a "professional"; they ought to know how to look after themselves. It's not my business to poke my nose into someone else's psyche. It is nobody's fault if a lonely person lies awake at night thinking that they can substitute multiple endeavors with patients for their own needs.

Choices, however, abound. Surgeons with many skills and physicians with three pounds of brain in their skull have the world to explore and the resources to modify the expression of their desires.

CHAPTER 10

Competitiveness

I sat wedged in a second class compartment of the train rumbling through the night from Paris to Rome.

My companions snored around me: the large lady in slippers leaned on her husband's shoulders while he snored with his mouth open. Their hen blinked in her cage in the rack above their heads, and from time to time she cackled without getting a response from any of us. The young man with thin cheeks sat with his big round cheese beside him. The middle aged portly man was asleep in the corner having placed his grey felt hat, with red feathers in the brim like a shaving brush, carefully in the rack on top of my little suitcase. I sat hemmed in between the large lady and the hat owner, nursing my glass medical slides on my lap.

In those days, slides were large, three and a half by three and a half inches for good detail. These were my precious possessions showing seizure activity in the depths of the brain, obtained by special recording. Our research results in the hospital where I worked were probably unique in the field of epilepsy. This documentation of our work, showing how the brain is functioning in certain epileptic seizures, was the baby on my lap. The abnormality may be limited to a few millimeters of the brain, and we demonstrated the pathways and the detailed events. For us, each slide was a thing of great beauty.

I was on my way to Rome, invited to join a Round Table Symposium at the International Congress of Neurophysiology. This was part of the personal "breakthrough" that ambitious people wait for early in their careers.

Waking early next morning I walked along the river Tiber. I watched the sun rise over the bridges, and listened to the church bells, dreaming of Tosca as I gazed up at St. Michael the Archangel brandishing his sword on the top of St. Peter's. Controlling the excitement over old stones and stories, I switched to turn my thoughts to the professional meeting and to clothes. These had to be attended to because in London my slides had taken precedence over clothes. So I stepped into an elegant little shop and inquired in my primitive Italian for a "little black dress". Immediately the effusive dress-makers crowded about me with suggestions, and then knelt on the floor with pins in their mouths cleverly making minute alterations as I stood turning round and round at their direction.

We then met punctually in one of the Congress halls for a "dress rehearsal" of the Symposium. The eager Moderator of the Round Table bossed us around appropriately, and I thought I understood where I was to stand in the pecking order of the men who had gathered there from all corners of the medical world.

The rehearsal over, I quickly disappeared back into happy anonymity along the banks of the river Tiber.

Early next morning at the little dress shop, Madame pinned a red rose onto the black dress, and I then arrived in plenty of time for the conference, clutching my precious slides which were to electrify the 2000 or so attendees in the hall.

I sat next to a French colleague, who had befriended me on the previous day, noting that I talked French and probably realizing that I was no match for the dictatorial "moderator".

Emotions of a Physician

The meeting opened with drawn-out speeches of the introducers, which threatened to put half the audience to sleep. Finally it came to the turn of The Round Table, the "meat" of the morning. The Moderator started off and hogged far more of the time than had been allotted to him on the previous day. Each man then grabbed the microphone and spouted away as though he were the one and only authority in the field.

I was watching the clock. I tried to conquer my rapid heart beat. I tried to grasp the mike as it passed down the line. I tried to say: "Please put up my slides", but I lacked the courage to interrupt the flow of my verbally skilled colleagues.

The meeting ended. The crowd clapped. The projectionist came down from his cage at the back of the room and politely handed me back my slides. The Round Table participants went off in a bunch down the hall, chatting.

I learned that morning that you don't get anywhere without competing, and competing fiercely. Researchers in the "highest" field of brain function behave in the same way as journalists jostling at press conferences, or men in shirt sleeves shouting in the stock exchange. They employ the same tactics "automatically". No one sits with a red rose waiting for his or her turn to speak. There is no such thing as taking turns. Just jump in.

Work in the laboratory leads to maneuvering at the international conference table, and the one is closely dependent on the other. Some years later in America, I learned the Harry Truman phrase: "If you can't stand the heat, get out of the kitchen".

The underlying force of competitiveness is: "I win, you lose." The underlying force of aggression is also usually: "I win, you lose". However, the underlying force of drive is simply: "I win." It is less adversarial. It does not necessarily involve another person losing. It indicates working to reach a self-set goal, an achievement to overcome a certain internal weakness or to attain some longing and ambition within oneself; to climb a mountain and touch the sky, if only for one moment.

In many cases, the underlying driving force of ambition can be: "I win, you win", and this type of ambition leaves room for others as well as oneself to claim recognition and reward.

We might term these forces "theses", like working hypotheses, except that since they are usually unconscious and not overtly expressed, the motivation which underlies our professional activities is probably more rightly termed a force rather than a thesis.

If we devoted time to list the values whereby we desire to direct our actions, we might choose the: "I win, you win" path. However life is short, we are in a hurry and we rarely take that time. Urgency and the pressure of daily events sit heavily on our chest. Next Monday morning is the Board meeting. Next week is the Departmental meeting and the budget must be ready. Next month is the Conference and the statistical analysis of our results is not yet done. Few of us sit down to examine our competitiveness. Few of us seem to preserve the vision that shone that night when we looked up at the Milky Way.

An assortment of competitive activities within the medical profession tempts us. There is the ambition to be the "first" in a particular research in the natural sciences; the first to diagnose; the first to find a cure; the first to carry out a life-saving operation, or to found a university, or to set up an efficient organization for the delivery of health care.

We compete in our interactions at every board meeting and at every "team" conference.

The goal of "I win" is helpful in many ways. It can satisfy and content us as individuals; this in turn should prevent us from interfering in the affairs of others. It can lead to accomplishment. It can beat the sloth of getting up in the morning or in the middle of the night; or the weariness when a pile of tests sits on the desk awaiting interpretation; or the tediousness of sorting out statistical results for publication in the latest medical journal; or the despondency when the waiting room is crowded with patients who want you to certify them as unable to work; you have bright ideas as to how they could get better, but many are not interested.

The competitive professional needs drive. Does that include aggression?

I learned the difference between "aggression" and "drive" one afternoon in snowy February in the Midwest.

I was called into the professor's room to be given the results of the routine evaluation of my performance made by the department and colleagues in a leading medical institution.

The professor said to me: "Your work is very good but you lack aggression". I was given to understand that if I did not mend my ways, I was not welcome in that chosen field, which I loved.

I walked out of the room, silent. I passed the open doors along the shiny corridor, where eager-beavers poured over their instruments, their buzzing and their whirring, their ticking and their clicking, the disgorging of paper, the lists of figures, the mountains of reference books, and the passionate discussions in the hallways.

I stepped out into the snowy driveway between the walls of cement blocks. The street was full of men walking home carrying their dispatch cases and looking straight ahead. I thought to myself: "they all know where they are going."

I arrived at my front door, where the fir tree was hung heavy with snow, its branches leaning across the entrance. From time to time there was a plop as a ball of snow fell to the ground. It was that tall fir tree that had greeted me when I, a stranger to that land, was looking for a house to buy. In my own mind I bought the house before ever crossing the threshold, having fallen in love with the protector of the house.

I unlocked the door; I looked at the bookshelves and the empty fireplace. Then I sat down and cried. What had happened to the ambition that drove me across the Atlantic, that inspired me to pour over the books, that made me turn down invitations to join the friendly crowd of "party-goers"? Clearly I was a failure.

I was not living up to the expectations of either myself or of the medical world which had offered me this golden opportunity for the acquisition of knowledge, and the discovery of truths; this "prestigious" position to save the sick and to teach the upcoming medical youth.

Three weeks later, I woke up one morning and said to myself: "What a fool I am. I did not recognize the difference between "aggression" and "drive". The only real mistake was not to have seized the opportunity to discuss this difference with those high-minded people who were doing the evaluation."

Clearly I want to win; clearly I want to show to myself that "I can do it", whatever "doing it" means. If at the same time, my "winning" over circumstances fits into the ambitions of others, then the activity is even more worthwhile.

Doctors have competed with each other since time immemorial. The history of medicine is full of tales of physicians' rivalry at the bedside. We are competitive for diagnostic skills, feeling victors when we make the correct diagnosis. This probably touches our honor and ego more than anything else. If a physician or surgeon can show that the last man or woman to diagnose and treat the patient was wrong and that he/she is right, then he/she wins on several scores; on the score of: "I win, you lose", and on the score of: "I win in the estimation of myself". In addition he/she implies to the patient: "You win because I win".

Hence fierce competitiveness can arise in the law courts between expert witnesses. There can be cruel undercutting of the previous attending doctor, who was at a disadvantage because time had not revealed the diagnosis and it is easier for a later arrival to make a correct diagnosis. In the same way, bitter controversy can arise in the research field when one conclusion is shown to be untenable because of a subsequent chain of experiments and observations.

We compete for the approval and if possible for the admiration and affection of students and staff, and of patients and their families. When patients are dependent on our skills, we gain a sense of power. Apart from being rivals in diagnosis, we compete for experience. We continue to add to the list of patients whom we have treated for a particular disorder. We compete for the status of being an expert in a special field; for renown, let alone publicity; for popularity; for financial reward; for general recognition; and for the pleasure of bragging in the doctors' room. Most people like to indicate that they are always busy and constantly in demand. We are a resource that wishes to feel needed, to wield power.

How are we to harness our energies for good use of this spirit of competitiveness?

We could recognize early in our careers the order of our priorities for personal satisfaction in life. In what order do we rank the three great ambitions to obtain success in life: glory, power and riches? Most of us desire a measure of each of these, and even those taking the vow of poverty are attracted by the honor and glory of the vow. But what do we value for ourselves the most: glory, power or riches? For which of these will we make the most sacrifices? For which of these do we compete the hardest?

Since competition is inevitable in the practice of medicine, we must distinguish between drive and aggression, because the differentiation has practical consequences. Although a non-aggressive approach may not bring the rewards of fame, money and worldly status, it has other rewards.

I worked with a neurologist, Professor Roe, whom I admired for his wide vision, his generosity in sharing his experiences and his many commitments in the community. Because he delegated well, I, in a junior position, worked closely with the patients on a day-to-day basis and knew the details of the cases. I was therefore often able to suggest the diagnosis when we talked in the doctor's conference room. Ten minutes later at the bedside, Doctor Roe would announce this diagnosis as if it were he who had done the work, which was what satisfied the patient. My reward was to earn this professor's respect and practical support for many years, presumably because he trusted my judgement.

Similarly, to achieve the adoption of a policy can be more important than pride of authorship. For example, one may originate an imaginative policy and suggest it to colleagues before it is officially discussed; at the Board Meeting, the Chairman of the Department proposes this policy to the Board and it gets adopted. On occasions, a policy might be unpopular, in which case the Chairman may be able to "pull the chestnuts out of the fire" for the author.

A non-aggressive approach often sacrifices the professional persona for the person, but peace of mind may be preferred to aggrandizement. Not winning the competition can allow the author of ideas to remain a contented private individual rather than a powerful physician.

Whatever the outcome of drive and competition, various ingredients are required to combine in this field. First, as individuals, we need to rid ourselves of our hang-ups, our own fears, or chip-on-the-shoulder. We must voice our dreams in a convincing way. We need to acquire a sufficient degree of objectivity and generosity to share our dreams with other "competing" spirits. Then, as strategists, we must seize the opportunity to merge our ambitions and co-ordinate our activities.

The competitive drive to understand health and disease is a force of great value. If the "I win" is reached at the price of an aggressive "you lose", then interpersonal relationships suffer and the art of medicine is debased. However the "I win, you win" situation, if skillfully addressed, can be achieved.

CHAPTER 11

The Acceptance of Change

"I have to change. That was ten years' work, but it didn't work out. The results of surgery are poor and we have to do something else. We have to start again."

A surgeon, Professor Field, spoke those words.

I was working one summer in Oxford to learn the specialized technique of peripheral nerve examination and analysis. Professor Field was in charge of the long-term project.

The patients had suffered nerve injuries from trauma, usually war wounds. They were examined at regular intervals over many years in order to study the results of suture of their peripheral nerves, mainly the large sciatic nerve in the thigh. Meticulous suturing of these nerves had been carried out by Professor Field and his surgical team, hopeful that recovery would restore function and improve the quality of life of the injured. Each operation took many hours, and the planning, evaluation and analysis was spread over several years.

As the data piled up, the hours of hope and work were seen to disappear into years that would be buried and forgotten. The observations that I and others brought to Professor Field that summer re-inforced his previous fear and sadness that his team's efforts had probably not been worthwhile.

One afternoon we were sitting in Professor Field's library. The sun made patterns on the desk piled with charts, diagrams, drawings of nerves, surgical procedures, histograms, columns of figures, and my findings neatly drawn out on pictures of the human body. Body after body. And all in vain. Or maybe not quite in vain, but enough to make Professor Field look up at me and say quietly :

"That's ten years' work, and not really worth it."

He smiled and thanked me for my help. He politely asked me what was my next work project. He hoped that I had profited by at least learning anatomy with him.

At that moment I felt that I was part of a great profession, learning to enrich the pool of knowledge and to accept defeat. With a last look at the nicely bound books behind Professor Field sitting at his desk, I thanked him and closed the door behind me.

I had just witnessed the sadness of investing years of life in learning and performing an operation, only to see that the results were poor and not worth the effort. I also admired the man who accepted with dignity a "wasted" slice of life with change and obsolescence.

Many years later I realized the bitterness that Professor Field must have felt, even if he suppressed it. This was when I myself had worked for twenty years to perfect the technique of a procedure, and was watching that procedure gradually slip into obsolescence. I then understood the realities of change. Doctors are of necessity wedded to change and forced to be superseded. We are buried under the steamroller of time.

What is more scary to some people than change? On the other hand, what is more exhilarating than the discovery of new things, inevitably leading to change?

The art of medicine embodies this dichotomy and therefore this conflict in the personal life of a doctor. Our professional rewards (both the credit we give ourselves and the outward recognition by colleagues and society) come largely for discoveries, either of "pure" scientific phenomena, or in the field of diagnosis or treatment.

These very discoveries, however, all too often lead us to become outmoded (quickly or slowly), and we are then confronted with the problem of discarding our vested interests in the ideas, theories and methods to which we previously adhered. "I worked on my experiments for ten years: don't tell me now that I could have done something else, and come to a different conclusion."

Even in disappointing experiences such as these, we understand the lure of looking for "discoveries", with new data to add sparkle to the humdrum routine of daily life. This is part of our addiction to change, to search, to discovery.

Doctors are likely to seek the challenge of making discoveries early in their career, and have to accept change in later life. Some doctors are temperamentally attracted to discovery. Discoveries are based on experiments, and these necessitate changes which may involve patients. Others are more unwilling to seek or advocate change and this difference will influence their type of practice.

Those who distrust change are more conservation-minded. They note that in treatment the passage of time alone may have inherent powers of recuperation. They warn us of the dangers of "experimentation" and remind us of the Hippocratic oath to "do no harm" and "leave well alone". Physiological checks and balances act as feedback systems within the body to maintain positive health.

Professional rewards come from satisfying patients who, as with doctors, are a population of mixed personalities from different cultures with varying traditions. Some like to be offered the "latest" gadget, the latest test and a new treatment. But when doctors suggest change in personal attitudes, habits and life style, people usually resist. When our daughter is about to marry a man with epilepsy, do we want to change our attitude and learn about seizures from our neurologist?

Patients usually welcome a physician who engages in the search for new knowledge, so long as the "experiments" are not carried out on themselves. But these same patients do not always realize that it is this quest for knowledge, ("newness") which is the mainspring of energy and zest for further confrontation with disease.

The exciting "top of the world" feeling filled me in the streets of Marseilles.

The early morning glowed with autumn sunshine, the pop-pop of the fishing boats' engines started up as they headed out of the harbor, with the V of blue water opening up behind the boat and the men arranging their gear. The plane trees shading the boulevards hung their "bobbles" from the branches; the church in the narrow Rue Paradis chimed the hour and called to the faithful. The café boys wiped the marble table tops.

Every day, the first cup of coffee and the croissant brought the excitement of the thought: "What shall I learn today ?" The lab will give up the secrets of why a seizure starts, how, when, where, with what, and why not?

What child does not ask WHY? And here, just by walking along the sunny streets with the fresh autumn breeze, I could open Pandora's box and the gnawing questions might be answered. No need to go to the oracle of Delphi: the cats in the laboratory and the patients in the hospital would give the key to open the door. Maybe not quite wide open, but anyway a start. We would still have to follow the maze to the Minotaur, but at least we had a thread as a guide. Just walk a bit faster and we will get "there". Experience taught me that each new hill climbed brought into view a new horizon, so that like Alice Through the Looking Glass we have to run faster in order not to fall behind. But we could at least feel that the race was a lot of fun and worth running.

The experience of each new patient was like listening to a fairy story that gave insight into the workings of the magic brain. Each new squiggle on the moving paper as it rolled off the machine recording brain wave activity was the unraveling of a detective mystery.

In the long afternoons in the laboratory we tolerated the struggle with the electrical circuit when resistance interfered with recording, because we believed that the cat, the Marseilles cat who seemed to have more than nine lives, was just about to give us the secrets of his "thalamus", the way-station in the brain of sensation coming from all parts of the body.

We were learning the relationship of brain waves to behavior, to seizures, to alertness; we were discovering the subtle changes during different activities. No wonder we worked till the moon was high in the sky, and the streets of Marseilles held only nocturnal wanderers with the town cats lurking in the corners.

I learned another lesson in Marseilles, the pain involved in change. I witnessed the difficulty that eminent scientists have in letting go of their personal theories and in accepting change. It nearly fractured their personalities. Maybe this is termed "ego grief". Whatever it is, it created a rumpus at the International Symposium with which I was closely involved, when our team was hosting this gathering of world-wide "authorities".

The participants were discussing the occurrence of episodes of altered behavior, with concurrent electro-encephalographic (EEG, or brain wave) alterations, which certain patients with epilepsy may manifest. These episodes of disturbed behavior are not directly related in time to a seizure; their occurrence is now commonly accepted by the scientific community, but this was the pioneer demonstration that such events occur.

At the meeting neurologists, psychiatrists and neuro-physiologists were discussing whether, when and how patients experience these aberrations, with mood change and often emotional outbursts. Being a neophyte in this subject at the time, I found it easy to accept; it was new and convincing, and furthermore my Professor was a leading champion of these new ideas, so that I admitted to local bias. But I witnessed the passionate arguments that raged in every meeting, and continued at the nightly gathering over wine and walking along the harbor quays where the fishermen were quietly laying out their nets to dry.

It was life and death to these scientists and doctors, talking away like the Tower of Babel. Many were severely upset by this confrontation with change, and they were struggling with their vanity, their life-blood, their previous creeds and attachments.

Emotions of a Physician

How painful is change! Emotional tension ran high, and change on that occasion was not accepted with the dignity that Professor Field showed. This Symposium taught me that there are many occasions in life when observations ("discoveries") lead to change, often uncomfortable for ourselves or for those who follow in the field.

Ten years after the work in Marseilles, we were studying patients with epilepsy, trying to apply to the human brain some of what we had learned from laboratory work with cats. We worked with neurosurgeons who added their skills to ours. In the operating room in a London hospital, I and my colleagues stood for many hours at our instrumental equipment recording "exciting" events from the brain as the surgeon operated.

Would we suddenly see a startling new brain wave? Would the electrical wave be square instead of the previously recorded pointed one? Because nobody had yet recorded the cerebellum (the hindbrain) during surgery, would the uncharted sea show that the world was round and not flat?

When we showed our results to a senior colleague, he commented:

"Well, at least you are not recording the rumblings of London buses passing in the street."

He was not going to commit himself as to any significance of new observations which might require him to change his views, but at least he acknowledged that the squiggles indicated true brain waves, and were not artifacts. What a glow of pride I felt ! I was indeed recording true phenomena and joining the ranks of the discoverers. I was causing change.

Seven years later, the monkey whom I named Alpha, was sitting in his chair in a spacious laboratory in the Midwest. Every day as I opened the elevator door, I would hear his high-pitched squeak of recognition, although he was in a room three corners away from the elevator. What alertness to vibration !

We would sit together, monkey and I, playing stimulus-response games day after day, eagerly awaiting the next discovery. Alpha would close his eyes in seeming contentment when I stroked his nose. He would fold his hands on his lap when I continued to stroke.

We would work together in the quiet room without any medication, so that his reactions would be as natural as circumstances allowed. He showed me that his responses to light or to sound differed according to whether the stimulus was given together or separately, and according to his moods. We recorded how the whole of his brain responded and not only the part specialized for reception of that particular stimulus. But each part had a significantly different response, a special signature tune.

Maybe one could have predicted all this, but predictions require proof. It will stand as "truth" until the next experimenter publishes results that bring change. Each evening when the experiment of the day was finished, I would sit reading a book next to Alpha the monkey, for company. Alpha usually went to sleep.

At the time when one team is making discoveries, other people will have to make changes, and adjust to new ideas.

Change is therefore the corollary of research; it is the inevitable result of discovery. We often enjoy hearing about discoveries. Many doctors rush off to meetings with a child's curiosity for the startling and the new. They may neglect spouses and families to work late in the laboratory and disappear to the library at weekends to write papers with the hope of becoming famous for their "discoveries".

The irony is that these very "discoveries" leading to change make us all out of date very quickly. The inbuilt senescence of medicine is obvious to society. But it is often hard for doctors to give up the pet theories that they or their teachers held only recently.

"That's nothing new, we showed that in 19—."

"That's still unproven, you need more data."

Also when ideas become outmoded, incomes derived from a surgical procedure that took years of research and training to achieve can be lost in a few months.

We cling to what we know and cannot easily exchange one piece of knowledge for another. Change in attitude is even harder to achieve than change in technique.

The acceptance of change involves handing over to the next generation, which may be unpalatable. Are we automatically jealous of our pupils, our successors? Do our children rival us? Looking to the future demands a generosity of spirit, somewhat rare in human beings.

Doctors welcome younger colleagues who will lift off the burden of night calls from them, and who will add income to their practice. But when the patients begin to favor younger colleagues because they are more open to new ideas, then bitterness may surface and grow.

Change per se is not necessarily "good" or "bad". But in the medical context, change follows discoveries from research and is inevitable. If we can accept change in our individual lives as desirable adaptation to discovery, we may be content with looking at things afresh.

CHAPTER 12

The Lure of Discovery

"Why do I have epilepsy?" Sabina asked anxiously, sitting on the edge of the chair. The sun backlighted her blonde hair which fell in ringlets to her shoulders. She would have been an attractive middle aged woman without that whining voice.

Why indeed did she have epileptic seizures? There was no clear genetic evidence of epilepsy; her birth was said to have been normal; and there were no significant illnesses in childhood. In her teens, she had "kept up" with her peers. On Friday and Saturday evenings, she and her friends would gather in pubs in cheerful groups and then after closure they would troupe to each others' homes, experimenting with alcohol and the available fashionable drugs.

"None of my friend have epilepsy, why do I?" asked Sabina in a strained voice. At the age of 22, she had had her first seizure on a Monday morning sitting in class at College. All she remembers is the embarrassment of waking up lying on the floor, with wet pants, and her frightened friends around her, saying, "What happened, Sabina?".

Her mother then took charge. She continued to live at home, and her parents were afraid of her going out alone at night. They took her to consult many doctors but she was silent at interview and hated the diagnosis of epilepsy. She had not married. Her clerical employment bored her but she was afraid to change jobs.

Sabina asked me again. "Why do I have epilepsy? Why me?"

I answered, "In your particular case, we may not show the exact cause, but we shall discuss the various possibilities. Epilepsy is a symptom, which has many causes. It is like the symptom of coughing, which arises from a number of different disorders. We can sort out which factor or which combination of factors come together at any particular time in your case to "fire off" the neurons into a seizure. Once you learn how and why the circumstances arise, and we find the right level of the appropriate medication to keep down the "firing" threshold for the neurons, you can chose your own way of life".

Sabina worked conscientiously, noting and reporting her activities and reactions, and we gradually narrowed down the potential triggers of her epilepsy. Finding the cause of one person's epilepsy does not provide answers to the fundamental why of the epilepsies as a whole, but for Sabina it led to her obtaining a driving licence and recovering her cheerful voice.

The nagging annoyance of not knowing WHY something happens, and the satisfaction when discovery of causation gradually emerges out of chaos, are the motivations that lure and keep doctors in the field both in research and in clinical practice.

"Why" is the oldest question in civilization. It is also the first question that many bright children ask, running endlessly after their exhausted parents, with the squeak of "Why?"

It was the lure of discovery and the offered carrot of research that took me across the Atlantic and brought me to America. I and my colleagues were given the opportunity to study the factors that influence epilepsy. How much oxygen does the brain need in different circumstances? And which part of this three lbs of brain is involved? How much does the cortex (the rind) need for metabolism as compared with the depths of the three lbs? Which part of these "deep", hidden parts are involved in any particular instance? How does this oxygen consumption vary during different circumstances? Does the brain need more or less oxygen during a seizure, as compared, for example, with times when the individual is making calculations, or sleeping and dreaming? What happens to oxygen consumption when a patients suffers a stroke? Many questions were buzzing in my brain as I sorted out mundane affairs of trans-Atlantic travel.

I sat in the cabin of the Queen Elizabeth liner, reading Kafka's novel Amerika and wondering if, like him, I would lose my suitcase as soon as I landed on "foreign" soil. It was little consolation to learn that Kafka described all these nightmarish mishaps without ever having set foot in America.

The dawn was cold; the snow made the deck slippery; the wind penetrated my thin coat. I stood with the dingy-looking crowd squashed on deck waiting for the statue of Liberty to make her appearance. The metal-bosomed woman finally emerged as a dot; and we were shuffled down to the bowels of the ship to line up for presentation of our immigration papers.

After moving slowly in the queue for an hour or so, I reached the grey uniformed men sitting at their tables.

As I stood awkwardly holding bags, packages and violin, I dropped the vital papers. The bulky man with metal medallions on his shoulders saw the "MD" on the floor written after my name. He remarked:

"Dropping papers won't make a good doctor!"

In the vast domed and echoing arena at New York docks, the crowd ran around shouting to gather together onto one spot their luggage, their children and the appropriate official for the "search". I realized that on this occasion it was easier to be alone. The next struggle was to find another official with the metal bands who would tie up my misshapen bags before I could be "passed" out to the world. The "world" at that moment was deluged in rain and presented another shouting match fighting for a taxi. No wonder I arrived, once I had found somewhere to lay my head, swollen with pride after "winning" the hurdle race.

The lure of discovery! This was what tempted Pandora to open her box, and what tempted me to try a new country. Curiosity is not curiosity if one knows the answers before carrying out the experiments. I was launched on the road of the New World, in the land of equal opportunity, the land where "nothing is impossible". We were on our way to discover great things about oxygen in the brain, in epilepsy and with strokes. New horizons would open up new ideas.

Together with medical discoveries related to functioning of the brain came the experiences of day-to-day functioning in unfamiliar circumstances. Part of the price of discovery is the need to adapt to uprooting and re-planting in new soil.

"Hi!" said the secretary working away at her shiny desk. I could never bring myself to say "Hi!". I knew that my "good morning" sounded stiff, prim and caricaturishly English, but I could not be sincere in these chameleon adaptations. Always smiling, the secretaries smiled more than the situation seemed to warrant, but then everything was more.

The day started with the squeeze into the elevator, and the hours were parcelled-up into hundreds of trottings, picking up that message, going to see that X-ray, arranging for that family conference, on time for that meeting, late for that seminar, Grand Rounds missed, telephone call not answered, tubes blocked, probes stuck, transistors changed and computers "down". Throughout it all a smiling face on top of a white coat. How interesting, how wonderful, how challenging, what a plunge into the campaign of making great discoveries.

"Do you want to see the Receiving Room of the hospital?" asked one of my young colleagues. "Certainly," I replied. So we descended to the bowels of the hospital in this great metropolis. Along dark corridors, close-packed on benches lining the wall, sat the black and white people, waiting. Here, this "abdominal emergency" had waited four to five hours, I looked at the card the elderly man held with the stamp of his checking-in time. This young man with complex psychiatric neurological symptoms, who had "done the rounds" before, sat here for eight to ten hours. This girl with a fever of 103° F waited thirteen hours and died undiagnosed.

Upstairs in the Conference room I had been shown the splendid statistics displaying the 400 adults who were examined per day and directed to the "right" department, and an equal number of babes and children who reached their appropriate niches. But what happened if you fell through the cracks?

The masses came because they had no family physician, because their slum homes were not the places where anybody went to make a diagnosis. They came because there was no alternative to the dark corridors of the Emergency department. And so the depersonalised "they" sat on benches.

"Do you wish to see the 'prisoners' brought in by the police?" my colleague asked. On stretchers, they lay chained with chains each link the size of a fist, and a chain across the stretcher (called the cart). Turning eyes of perforated peptic ulcers, acute fevers, or ulcerated corneas, I felt their silent gaze. In a separate chamber, behind a barred-up grill, sat an adolescent black girl in a peacock-blue sweater with a chain from her ankle to the floor; beside her an elderly black woman squatted chained to the floor. I remembered the goats in France beside the road. But here were fellow human beings with dehumanized eyes.

By the back gate of the glistening University hospital were decaying brick buildings labelled "Hotel", with broken windows, at which black figures stood staring. It began to drizzle. I stepped over a rat. It had probably been there three days: the first day by a little pool of blood, the second with swollen abdomen and bloated, and the third decomposed. The series of cases published from that university of Weil's disease (human illness carried by the infected urine of rats) were shockingly impressive, because most places do not have the opportunity to study this disease.

I asked:

"What are the houses built of?"

"Wood, with some bricks and mortar." It was a maze of shacks, twisted fences, broken verandahs, State incinerators and Coca-Cola bottles which do not burn. Wicker chairs and couches disemboweled their stuffing in the rain; black figures wheeled carts piled high with boarding, car tires, rags and bones, cardboard boxes — do they sell or burn?

In every corner stood the bashed-in, tawdry, tinny, vast automobiles, the only spots of color in the thin misanthropic rain, with their bent bumpers lined up outside houses which may or may not have been inhabited.

Men, in grimy loud tartan shirts, crouched in shacks or tents beside their cars, came out to watch us. They looked as though they were on the "road West" but they were clinging on here, caught, imprisoned in this wet slum. Perhaps our "civilization" would have done better to have left them in their slums in the sunny South, with swollen abdomens from deficiency diseases, rather than entice them to travel North and become exposed to acute yellow atrophy of the liver from polluted rats' urine.

I crossed the street to photograph a wooden "house" where the lady on her doorstep was keeping up her self-esteem with high heels. Neighbor groups formed, broke-up and re-formed. Suddenly out came an angry woman dressed in turquoise and started gesticulating and shouting at us. My colleague whispered: "Let's go!" So I retreated into the car and we drove off quickly. We passed the street corner with the shell of a shop and glass littered all over the road, gutted.

Discovery is often more meaningful when the context of the discovery is known. I wanted therefore to learn something of the lives of our patients. Observations take on deeper meaning if the more general picture is understood.

However I was barred from entering those broken-down houses. I was not welcome to my patients' homes, because I clearly belonged to a different world. But I tried to make my own observations as far as circumstances allowed. The consumption of oxygen by the brain may not depend on social factors, but the occurrence of high blood pressure and strokes is part of people's way of life.

The lure of discovery, the urge to unearth facts and to imprint one's personal stamp in any particular field is similar in all professions, and indeed in all human activities. In the medical profession, it is expressed by curiosity in "how things work", in how the body reacts to the ever-changing environment, and how psycho-physical humans change over the years in different circumstances.

I changed in those years of new experiences, because I tried to incorporate insecurity and to see the funny side of failure. When I locked myself out of the apartment or took the wrong back alley on the way home, I tried to smile like many of those suffering heroically in bleak houses. I learned that many factors influence outcome, particularly attitude.

Predicting is an unreliable art, and yet the medical profession is constantly demanded to predict. "How will this illness turn out, Doctor? Shall I live or die, and if I am to die, how soon?" These questions can lead medical practitioners to having a sense of power, dangerous and fallible, and yet the doctor cannot escape this responsibility.

The doctor's role in present Western society is shifting to education: encourage people to learn the patho-physiological facts, and to make the choices themselves of how they wish to live. With a modicum of affluence, choice is available. (Without that modicum, it is not, in which case social factors are of primary importance.)

During the educational stage of handing over personal responsibility to people, the boundaries are fluid and conflicts arise. However, before responsibility can be shared out between doctor and patient, the doctor has to understand where the patient is coming from, what is their habitat and their present background. What was appropriate for me to do and to think in the past was no longer appropriate in my present situation. I therefore had to set out to make further discoveries.

Doctors with curiosity will continue to seek, consciously or unconsciously, difficult situations in which to make new discoveries.

Sabina had said: "Why do I have epilepsy?" "Why me?" Why indeed. There is always something more to find out. The one thing that keeps doctors going, that never lets a doctor down, is intellectual curiosity.

CHAPTER 13

Instant Gratification and Infant Omnipotence

One Saturday evening I stood in a dark little room on the 7th floor at the top of a tenement house in Edinburgh. The portly grandfather, Mr. McPherson, lay on a truckle-bed gasping for breath. His swollen legs pitted when I pressed them with my fingers, and his swollen abdomen full of fluid resonated like a drum when I percussed it. Mr. McPherson's middle-aged daughter stood silently by the stove near the bed. In the dim light, I could just make out the parrot looking down at me from his perch.

It was my first meeting with Mr. McPherson, but acute heart failure was an easy diagnosis. No history needed, no test required. I whipped open the black bag, drew up the fluid in the syringe, placed the old gentleman's arm comfortably stretched out on the bed, and injected slowly and steadily into the vein at the elbow.

Oh the wonders of medicine! Mr. McPherson's breathing eased up; he turned his face towards me, grinned and asked his daughter for a cup of tea. "Thank you, Doctor", he said, as I closed my bag. His daughter gave me a shy smile as she watched the kettle.

Next day, I climbed the steps of the seven floors expectantly and opened the door. The parrot turned his head and squawked "Hello". I lifted the bedclothes; the swelling of the legs was down, and the abdomen was no longer tight as a drum. Oh! the instant gratification that flooded over me: know-how, action, praise, satisfaction, justification for having been called out on a Saturday and missing the party with my friends.

Immediate gratification is frequently needed by patients, and this is understandable in many cases.

Emotions of a Physician

People usually wait to consult a doctor until anxiety has risen to a degree of emotional tension so that the kettle is boiling over. In cases of acute injury and sudden illness, or in chronic situations when people finally make up their mind to act, patients have a sense of urgency. This need for immediate gratification is transmitted to the doctor, and in many situations is shared by the doctor. Quick results give early satisfaction and earn praise. However, experience teaches how to evaluate immediate needs, and sometimes instant gratification needs to be resisted.

My physician friend, Marvin, in a large multi-specialty clinic, had an ardent desire for immediate information. Marvin wanted blood sugar results to be available to him almost instantly. Treatment should be more effective with blood sugar data at hand. However, this led Marvin to demand immediate results on an ever-increasing number of chemistry tests.

A flurry of meetings was organized; we met at 7 AM so as not to interfere with hospital in-patient work; and pressure for quick results of every possible test was pushed down the line to the laboratory staff.

I watched Marvin standing at the ward telephone, calling up the lab, drumming his fingers on the desk, tapping with his feet, and with his eyes roving, while the ward clerk was waiting impatiently to use the phone for other purposes. I could visualize the lab clerk at the other end running to the lab technician who would then drop a pipette and rustle through the computer type for the required results.

The cascade of hurry, hurry, hurry streams through the system, and everyone goes home with a headache.

Marvin was a Mennonite of Russian origin from the plains of Kansas, who described his childhood urge for action, and his struggle to move out of a restricted life into the freedom of a competitive society. He had piercing blue eyes, a rigid neck and a manner that implied: "I am going to win this battle."

With a passionate love of achievement, Marvin would look at me and say :

"In a Veteran's hospital, you wait for a result for a month; in a University hospital you wait a week, and in private practice less than a day."

Immediate gratification is appropriate in some circumstances, and I was inspired by Marvin's eagerness and his total devotion to patients.

Not many years later, I stood with my colleagues in church on a cold February day, mourning along with many patients, at Marvin's funeral service. Marvin had died from stress-related collagen disease.

Our desire for instant gratification accelerates life, and we may gain short-term successes and rewards from our patients. However, when the race in life progressively speeds up, we may reach the milestone of death sooner than we would otherwise.

On the one hand, push-button medicine now available in many areas is a significant advance for numerous conditions. With a quick test, a computerised answer and a program instituted to prevent complications, we can alleviate fears. This is in contrast to "the bad old days" when we might wait until it was too late.

On the other hand, it is wise to ask: Is that instant gratification translated into greater general contentment? Do the two advance hand in hand? If the time gained is not pleasantly employed, what was the point of hurrying?

We all need to see the result of our work. And the sooner the better. In addition, doctors are aware that life may be cut-off at any moment, and therefore (consciously or sub-consciously) they desire results to follow actions with as short a delay as possible.

Is patience something that grows with age? No. Is patience a quality that increases with the years of medical experience? Yes, but only in some cases.

The patient has much the same reactions as the doctor, with even greater pressure for quick results. Doubt as to the diagnosis must be instantly removed. Delay is probably the most intolerable situation for a patient to experience. Pain must be immediately relieved. Unpleasant experiences must be made to pass quickly.

"Get going! for God's sake DO something! Doctor," And that "Get going" with the gratification of action is followed by the need to observe rapid results.

People delay going to see the doctor for the first time, hoping that the symptom will disappear, but once the responsibility for decision-making has been transferred to the physician, then the pile-up of anxiety, and the need to lift that anxiety translates itself into pressure for immediate results. Instant gratification is expected as a result of the doctor's activity, and he/she in turn derives gratification from taking a situation in hand.

Throughout many years of medical practice, rapid action would give me and my colleagues a "high".

When on call, I often awoke hearing the ambulance bell ring as it passed my house on its way to hospital.

One night the telephone rang from the Emergency Room: a patient with a head injury from a snowmobile accident was expected to be brought in soon. The emergency doctor and I (the neurologist) met on the doorstep.

George, a young man, was semi-conscious and restless; there was blood coming from one of his ears; the pupils were unequal; he was moving all four limbs and his airway appeared intact. The friend who accompanied him told me that George ran slap into a tree trunk on his snowmobile while driving around in the moonlight.

His neck moved freely, but as we were examining him, he responded less and less to alerting stimuli, and the blood pressure was rising. The team went into action: the electro-cardiogram was done, blood was typed so as to be compatible, the blood chemistry was taken, the intravenous fluid was in place, and the operating staff was alerted. With the patient's level of consciousness going down, I telephoned the neurosurgeon, and told him that I diagnosed a subdural hemorrhage from the nature of the injury and the neurological state of the patient.

Within a matter of minutes, brain surgery was started, the subdural hemorrhage was stopped, the blood clot removed and George recovered without any deficit.

Next morning, he was sitting up in bed. He grinned at me and said:

"I guess you saved my life, Doctor. My friend told me it was a pretty near thing; thank you."

It is gratifying words like these that draw ambitious medical students to surgery.

The reward of gratification comes to all doctors at various times, but immediate gratification is more often available to surgeons. The first inflamed appendix, lying like a red worm amongst the loops of bowel, removed at 2 AM before it perforates, is heady wine to the young surgeon. Some years later, in order to achieve the same feeling of accomplishment, the surgeon requires a more unusual event, for example, a television appearance introducing him or her as the first operator to do a particular transplant in a remote city.

A physician's gratification is likely to be achieved for work done at a slower pace than a surgeon's. With long-term treatment, one awaits long-term results.

A Southern gentleman, Samuel, with a slow speech and an accent that sounded like a Louisianian was admitted to hospital in a wheelchair. He put his broad-brimmed hat down carefully on the table beside the bed. He had long legs and even as he lay in bed I noted that they were bowed, presumably from many years of horseback riding. He had come to hospital alone, and his blue eyes were enquiring. He had had a stroke and could not walk.

Samuel met me with a smile; and every day he thanked the nurses; he obeyed the physical therapists; he put all the square blocks into square holes as taught by the occupational therapists; he listened to all the do's and don'ts of posture, feeding and psyche, usually so annoying to receive for the person recently deprived of their independence.

"I have to learn that all my daily activities, previously automatic, now take five times as long to carry out as they did before. Yes, I understand that frustration merely retards my improvement. However, I can dream of my farm in the deep South, my horses, the open spaces, the big sky, my cattle waiting in the corral," he said.

One day, Samuel received a letter from his wife of 40 years, saying that she was leaving him. After he told me the news, we still went ahead and planned his return to the South, with self-help appliances. We waved him good-bye at the hospital gate.

Six months later, Samuel walked into my neurological office, with a cane and a smile, just to say "Hello and thank you". He brought a photograph of himself sitting on his bay horse in the sun with the cattle standing nearby. We chatted, and felt deep pleasure that afternoon.

Next week I heard from the local hospital. Samuel, who had taken the opportunity to come and thank me when he came North to attend the funeral of an old friend, had fallen by the church door and fractured the femur of the previously stroked-out lower limb. He was therefore starting again on the long road of rehabilitation.

Ten months later, Samuel sent me a Christmas card with the same bay horse and a message of hope.

When our patients teach us patience, can we drop the urge for instant gratification? Can a gardener plant and wait for the coming of next Spring?

Infant omnipotence is a near relative of instant gratification. Omnipotent denotes having unlimited power or authority. Long acquaintance with the wives of many doctors has taught me that this behavior of infant omnipotence is a frequent cause of friction in the home.

Craig always expected his wife to find his papers or keys or brief case for him. He would leave them in unlikely places, such as the closet under the stairs when he came home late at night. Sally his wife had an eye for finding mislaid objects, and the losing habit did not at first seem important. Gradually, however, Craig began to expect her to pack his suitcase whenever he went to meetings, to remind him of all engagements and to look after his every need. She only began to resent it when he became impatient and shouted round the house like a two-year-old.

The omnipotent person implies that: "I can sit in the middle of the room like a two-year-old expecting the world to revolve around me. I have that power and the household will do my bidding; if not, I shall scream. My secretary will call up the next patient. My nurses will lay out the tray for the next procedure. The team will wait for me, because nothing can happen till I arrive".

Whether husbands of women doctors suffer the same aggravation is less obvious.

To be in a position of power is both scary and gratifying. A trained doctor is supposed to be capable of action based on specific information. Eve has eaten the apple that the serpent gave her, and with this act of disobedience she has gained knowledge which gives power. As a physician I need to trust my own powers, because otherwise I cannot convey trust when I walk into the Emergency Room to treat, for example, a man with a stroke or delirium tremors from acute alcohol intoxication.

Instant Gratification and Infant Omnipotence

The day I was called to see a woman who had swallowed Ajax, I had no prior experience to rely on, but I used authority to call the Poison Center and gather a team to set up acute dialysis. I need sufficient confidence to have plenty to share with that scared five-year-old who has just fallen out of a hayrick; that acting-out teen-ager who puts up a bold front; that anxious old lady who fears to face the unknown kingdom of death.

A good leader has power and authority. How do we travel the road of the unmapped country unless we have faith in our map-reading? It is true that the final drop over the edge of the world into nothingness is done by the patient alone. However, every other step can he assisted by a leader who is visible out in front or walking along in the rear, available when required.

Power in the sense of control is the key to the sensation of "all-rightness". The feeling of being in control of the situation should be shared by all concerned, physician, patient and relatives. However, it is easy for the balance to be tipped, so that the doctor takes on the major share and assumes a mantle of omnipotence. There is then the danger that this behavior may regress to that of an infant sitting on the floor, infinitely omnipotent.

I worked with a surgeon, Dr. Kronski, who was famous for his gall-bladder operations, where the technique is often difficult, partly because of the danger of cutting the gall-bladder duct.

One day in the operating theatre, I was assisting at surgery, holding the retractor on the gall-bladder. As I peered down into a dark hole of the abdomen, gently clinging on an instrument for half an hour, with the exact amount of tension required for a living organ, my hand began to ache. My tired fingers moved a millimeter or so.

"Don't move!" cried Dr. Kronski. I re-adjusted my fingers.

"Retractor, Nurse".

"No, not that one, my special one, Nurse".

For some reason, the particular instrument could not be found immediately that day on the operating tray. Kronski's voice rose several frequencies.

"Head light, Nurse." The nurse delegated to fix the surgeon's light throughout the operation, instantly adjusted the head piece. Meantime the desired instrument was produced.

A few minutes later, there was blood in the dark hole.

"Suction!" It was done. After suction had cleared the operating field, when calm seemed restored, order followed contradictory order till Dr. Kronski snapped:

"Don't do nothing till I don't tell you!"

In the end, the patient fared well, but everyone in the operating room had been called every name under the sun and reduced to small stature.

Day after day, the operating staff witnessed a similar show. Many resented the petulance but some took it calmly, knowing that the less they reacted, the shorter the emotional display.

Dr. Kronski could have obtained better results and not lost the respect of the team if he had refrained from behaving with infant omnipotence.

Instant Gratification and Infant Omnipotence

After medical training and many years of daily responsibility, and being established in society with the cloak of self-righteousness, a doctor is unlikely to visualize him or herself as a petulant infant.

In addition, it may be difficult to resist the pleasure of receiving the attention and affection that surrounds a small child. At any age, we enjoy being petted and fussed over when we come home after a long day's work. People, however, are not going to continue playing into the game of infant omnipotence. And if gratification is to be long-lasting, it will come not from external events; it will come from inner equanimity.

CHAPTER 14

Status: Fashion and Fluctuations

I had a Russian colleague, Ivan, with a brilliant mind for discussing the intricacies of the mechanism of epilepsy, who was a delight to meet over a cup of coffee in the doctors' room. His erudition and entertaining conversation were such that, whether at 11 AM on a Monday morning or at 11 PM, one was enraptured by his company.

Ivan was also not afraid to show his own insecurity, his intellectual doubts about the latest neurological theories and about his place in society. His mother had dreamed of her son getting out of one strata of society and blossoming at a higher level. Her one desire was for her son to climb out of the back streets of New York and make a name for himself in the world of Fifth Avenue or to become President of at least one organization. Ivan's father toiled as a waiter; his mother gave her working life to dressmaking for the wealthy. Together they struggled for their son "The Doctor" and throughout his youth Ivan was reminded of the fact.

One summer's day Ivan invited me to come sailing with him and his parents in the boat that he had just acquired. He thought that I knew more about sailing than I did, and maybe he hoped that I would help him make a favorable impression on his parents. We all assembled at the lake. We managed, more by luck than good management, to set sail, Ivan, his father and mother and I. Ivan's wife chose to sit in the sun on the shore with their little girl.

First the sail could not be hoisted; then the wind rose and the sail had a mind of its own. The boom got out of hand; there were conflicting proposals as to procedure, no-one daring to take charge. The boat began to lean suspiciously. Ivan's father criticized his son; Ivan's mother changed from admiration to panic; Ivan had little idea what to do and I was not skilled enough to take charge. The boat tipped more precariously; we heard the little daughter crying out to her mother on the shore. Finally in one short minute we were all spilled out into the cold lake water. Indignity mixed with fear supplied energy enough for us all to reach shore, holding on to Ivan's mother from New York, whose distress was greater than my unhappiness at the plight of my crestfallen colleague Ivan.

We dried on the beach, trying to make light of wet clothes and waste of a sunny Saturday. That evening I joined Ivan's entire family for supper in a noisy restaurant where we crunched popcorn on the floor underfoot. Throughout the steak and salad meal, I tried to build up Ivan's status with his parents. But status is hard to restore in front of one's parents, after they have been invited to admire a newly-wealthy owner who tips them out of his boat.

That evening I thought about what status means to oneself, one's family and friends, and as a doctor to the public. Many viewpoints must be considered so as to build up a composite picture of the status of doctors in society at any particular period of time and in any particular culture. It is like looking at a sculpture: people walk all round the sculpture and each one sees it at a different angle: one person sees the feet, one looks up at the face, one is only interested in the material, wood, stone or marble from which the image is sculpted.

Emotions of a Physician

What is status? It can be described as one's place in society. The *Oxford English Dictionary* defines status as: "social or legal position or condition; rank, prestige; superior social position, etc". There are at least two viewpoints of this situation. The first is one's own view of oneself. How does the doctor see his or her own place in society? And the second is how does the public (and in this case how do the patients) see the place of the doctor?

The viewpoint of the family members of physicians and surgeons is colored by the doctor's own image of his or her place in society. Do I drop my professional persona with my medical bag at the front door, or do I carry it into the home? The fact that work overflows into the home, with telephone calls and beepers carried, and that the hours of work or being on call are variable, makes professional life spill into personal life more than with certain other professions. This adds to the difficulty of taking off the professional cloak in homes. Unless I separate work and home life consciously, anxiety concerning patients and worry that the "right" thing has not been done distorts my personal vision. It also carries the danger of making me pompous.

Status is perceived differently according to the eye of the observer. A physician's status may not look the same to nurses and other health care staff; to actual or potential patients; to people who have never yet had personal experience of doctors; to politicians and planners who meet physicians on organizational matters, and to lawyers who work with or "against" doctors in management cases. Can we resist holding opinions only out of personal experiences?

Status: Fashion and Fluctuations

How do doctors perceive their status? This has fluctuated widely down the ages. During the past 150 years, even before the modern era, five major discoveries changed the face of medicine and therefore the status of doctors. These discoveries were: (1) of micro-organisms ("microbes", the causative agents of many diseases), by Louis Pasteur working intensively from 1850 onwards and announcing his famous germ theory in 1878; (2) surgical anesthesia with ether by William Morton in 1846; (3) the development of aseptic surgery arising from Joseph Lister's application of Pasteur's experiments; (4) Robert Koch's demonstration (1882) that the tubercle bacillus caused tuberculosis, which led the way to causation of infectious diseases, and (5) the discovery of antibiotics by Alexander Fleming in 1940.

Prior to these discoveries, the art of medicine consisted largely of diagnosis and prognosis of the "natural" course of illness followed by supportive treatment of the individual. This support required the doctor to have an "aura" and personal magnetism, and for the doctor and patient to build up mutual faith and emotional bondage. The supportive work was also shared with religion.

Modern medicine brought a different and stronger power over life and death events into the hands of the medical profession, and therefore changed the status of doctors. Fear, hope, trust, and public observations of wonders mixed with wild dreams entered the field. Thus the ambition to gain control over "all" things hit both doctors and patients. Fashion put the doctor on a pedestal.

With the twentieth century revolt, in all fields, against authority and authoritarian figures, the balance of dependence and independence shifted again, involving status change. Shared information, patient education and sophistication has now removed the pedestal from under the feet of physicians. They now stand on their own legs, in a more realistic light of day.

Because unrealistic evaluation of status by the on-looking public is diminishing, the doctors' own internal feelings of self-worth and their place in society becomes a more potent factor in the overall picture of status. We are all more together in the market place than before. It should be more comfortable than before, except that all change brings with it the need of flexibility, not always easy to appreciate.

How do these historical fluctuations affect the doctor's own feelings of status?   History is not wiped out by change.   Various parts of the world change at different rates, so that when the doctor works in different cultures, he or she may meet contradictions.

Status is often linked to heroic deeds. We read the stories of heroism when doctors and nurses walked the streets treating plague, or mixed with cholera patients, or lived in leprosy colonies. We are aware of doctors involved in wars throughout history. We add involvement with famine, drug abuse, unwanted pregnancies and auto-immune-deficiency-syndrome to the long list. The opportunities for "heroism" depend on our perception of heroism. To some observers, heroes seem to drop status.

The unsung hero may be in the back streets of low income areas; or treating diseases brought on by the patients themselves who find it hard to understand this idea. The unsung hero may be the carrier of bad news and one who is powerless to improve the situation, so that the patient discharges his or her anger back onto the doctor.

It is important psychologically how I esteem my own worth (internal status), while external status, public estimation of one's work, in the form of public recognition, financial rewards, even desirability as a spouse, is less important. This, however, goes to the heart of personal values. And who does not need recognition in the form of overt reward for work ? Who is "above" feeling sad when one's own profession is publicly charged with bad practices and non-caring ?

On the other hand, who does not want to have a "nice" sounding career word to say when people ask you: "What do you do?". If you answer: "I work in the Tax Department," you may expect a look of antagonism.

One's estimation of oneself needs constant revision as far as the public goes. But the internal evaluation depends on the values that one either had in the past, probably at a very early age, or that one retained throughout a life of action and temptation, or that got lost in the shuffle.

Loyalty to ideas is usually not the same as loyalty to values. In addition, we have to consider change and mutation not only in people but in systems, in processes and in organizations, when we discuss the perception of status. When a medical "break-through" or an exposure of medical wrong-doing occurs, the individual doctor may feel personal involvement. This is similar to team loyalty, team identification. The "break-through" or the evil deeds are usually quite irrelevant to a particular doctor's status or self-worth. Yet an irrational emotion links the individual to the profession.

It is more important to consider the physician's private status. Do I wish to be elected President of this or that? Who does not? But do I misjudge the appropriateness of my personal ambitions? Do I forget that "qualifications" for any particular post include not only the quality of the work accomplished, but the public image required with considerations of the old boys' club or the old girls' network? These are the realistic politics of life, not always appreciated.

I learned this lesson when I applied for the post of consulting neurologist at a teaching hospital in London. I had the experience, the expertise, and the publications, but very little appreciation of the fact that I "looked" the wrong candidate. I was unaware of the fact that since Masons numbered many of the senior staff, a woman was persona non grata, and that a cotton dress was not compatible with the status of the job. Theoretically I understood that status was important for the public, but I was blind to the fact that this applied also to myself. For many years I resisted attaching any importance to status which arose from one's "image" in the eyes of others. I closed my ears when a colleague told me that people receive personal invitations because of what that acquaintance will bring to the practice.

Advances and changes in society often take place quicker and easier when people feel comfortable rather than uneasy, particularly if their uneasiness is based on illogical prejudice. Minor compromises, taking into consideration other people's preconceived image of, for example, a doctor, do not necessitate "selling one's soul" or abdicating that ambiguous ideal called freedom. Political aims do not imply utilizing unsavory means. We often learn this lesson too late in life.

Fashion, as applied to the practice of medicine, requires that patients feel comfortable with the physician. In any given society, at any particular period, there is a "norm" for a doctor's image, whether we like it or not.

The "norm" can and does modify, and doctors are likely to choose their future colleagues realizing the change, whether the rate of change be rapid or slow. When I failed to get the job in the London teaching hospital, I realized that the change that I was expecting from others was too uncomfortable to be acceptable. I went elsewhere and understood not to take it personally.

There is probably an inverse ratio between the need for status and the degree of self-esteem. The more unassailable the self-esteem, the less need for higher status in the eyes of the world. "Look at me" is a universal desire in the playground when the child slides down the chute or jumps off a high wall. None of us, with the child inside ourselves, lose this need for attention throughout life. The doctor is in a precarious state at nearly every turn. I, the physician or the surgeon, need to be taken seriously. I need to be listened to. I must be part of the decision-making process. I am someone who "counts." My family no doubt see me in a different light, but they like my financial support. If I am not respected by my patients and in the community, I lose my income, my status and my self-respect.

The feeling of status is private but what role do we in society play ? We need the reinforcement of society, and the feedback of approval. We are not lonely artists. We are not the genius in a back street. The days of Marie Curie, of individual discovery of radium, are over. You either get a grant or you can't carry on with your work. We may shun or seek publicity, but we cannot avoid being judged by the public. How much we allow that judgement to affect our personal contentment is a matter for constant assessment throughout professional life.

We can observe how much status in respect of public perception touches doctors personally when we stand in the witness box. It is difficult for us not to resent being accused of malpractice. Honor is wounded. The word honor is out of fashion, considered old-fashioned, but the deep sense of being accused falsely and of not being sufficiently appreciated is unchanged throughout the ages. In the nursery we were told not to pout and not to think of ourselves as "Little Miss understood". How in modern society is the physician to be understood? Is it easier to understand someone else than yourself? Doctors spend a good deal of their time trying to understand someone else.

Medicine occupies an important, sensitive place in society, and as doctors we play both a private and a public role. We therefore need to be aware of our public image, and of status with its fluctuating fashions. By our behavior, we help mold this image with its changes. At times, we need to modify or sacrifice our personal desires in the interest of this status; that does not involve sacrificing our ideals. It is good to remember and apply the Greek principle of "nothing too much."

CHAPTER 15

Imagination: The Gnomes and the Snake

Jo was a stocky little man, who had been a construction worker in Toledo, Ohio.

He had jumped into a dry dock in Korea by mistake, and been picked up unconscious with a head injury. Fate brought him to the Head Injuries Hospital in Oxford, where I met him.

He made jokes every morning when we did our hospital ward rounds, and we looked forward to his friendly face. He objected to the wet weather, to the lack of Coca-Cola, to Saturdays without TV baseball and to evenings without the Detroit Tigers versus the St. Louis Cardinals.

Poor Jo! He walked on a broad base, very unsteadily, and his eyes had a constant jelly-like wobble (nystagmus), but his staccato speech was improving, and he was the most cheerful member of the rehabilitation class.

One day he said to me:

"You know, Doc, this morning there were little gnomes sliding down the bannisters!"

I tried not to look surprised. I didn't think that construction workers indulged in making friends with gnomes.

"Yes", he went on, "they wore little peaked hats, red and green and there were sparklers like the ones we have at home on the fourth of July. They all sat on the top of the stairs and then came whizzing down the staircase railing."

I looked up at the old carved oak staircase, not however expecting such exciting scenes. I didn't have as good an imagination as my patient from Ohio.

Emotions of a Physician

It took me a little time to realize that he had been having a seizure as a result of his head injury.

After that, having realized that he was not losing his mind, Jo told us about more miniature people who came his way. They were his gnomes, and quite friendly. They would move rapidly, usually with bright lights "like magnesium"; they did not talk, but they smiled and waved their hands. At other times, the shaking leaves of the birch trees in the garden might turn into fairy-like figures.

Patients tend to tell nurses or speech therapists or students about their odd experiences, being afraid that doctors may think them "balmy" or "off their rocker". But when you inquire, as a matter of course, whether for example after amputation your patient can still move his amputated leg in bed, or wiggle the toes that were not there, you learn to enter in with people to their private world of oddities, and the "unreal" fuses with the "real".

Miriam was an old lady of 80, who had looked after her bachelor son for all his 50 years. One day he did not come home from work, and the police brought back his clothes to Miriam with the news that he had died suddenly in a London underground train. Next day a neighbor lady found Miriam lying on her kitchen floor with the left side paralyzed.

In hospital, Miriam felt more comfortable wearing her hat in bed, than with her wispy hair uncovered in the public ward. From the bed next to her on the left, Mrs. Roberts made pleasant little conversational remarks, and offered her a slice of fruitcake.

In the morning I visited Miriam. She sat up and adjusted her hat with her right hand.

"You know, Doctor, that lady is in bed with me under the bedclothes. Her legs are up against mine".

I looked at Mrs. Roberts who was quietly washing her face and luckily had not apparently heard the remark.

In due course, Mrs. Roberts went home, but next day Miriam again assured me that her neighbor was lying under the bedclothes with her. I hope that it made her feel less lonely.

One day, a car mechanic, Harry, telephoned the doctors' office to say that he was disturbed because suddenly that morning as he sat eating his breakfast by the window, the cars started to dash very fast across to the right hand side as he watched them. He did not think that he could go to work until: "this thing gets fixed."

I was worried, and went to see what was going on. As Harry sat in his chair, it appeared to him that the cars moved at the ordinary speed as they came into view on the left hand side. Then when they reached the mid line, they suddenly accelerated and rushed off to the right hand side. In addition, Harry told me that the large clock which had stood in the middle of the mantle piece for the past 30 years was moving off to the right hand side and kept nearly falling off the edge.

Harry had other signs of central nervous system disturbance, with impaired sensation and slight loss of finger dexterity, which he had not noticed because the car speeds were so all-absorbing.

I could reassure him that the clock and the cars would come back to "normal" behavior, but that we needed to try to prevent a stroke, and advised him to come into hospital that day.

These frequent encounters with peculiar events in the "real" world, more intriguing than the movies can depict, stimulated me to study the inhabitants of a State Hospital in Minnesota.

Patients are not infrequently admitted to a near-by State Hospital for mental disorders when they start behaving oddly, for example seeing things that are not there, or not recognizing people whom they have known all their lives. They may otherwise be going about their business as though nothing were amiss.

I began to get to know the inhabitants of the large brick building, standing in the green fields where the spotted cows munched in the sun.

The first man, Al, elderly and white-haired, came slowly and cautiously into the room. He took one look from the door and said in a deep voice:

"There's money on the floor".

He then bent down and tried to pick it up. I watched as he scratched the bare floor diligently. There were indeed round white spots on the floor the size of coins. They were the shadows from the Venetian blinds which were drawn .

When I could get Al to stop trying to collect money, we sat down to look at pictures. The cars did not interest him. But as soon as we found a page where he saw a nice brown cow, Al tried to stroke her haunches. He kept turning over the page to look on the other side for that smooth skin of his familiar cow.

After that, he settled down to tell me all about his cow Daisy, and we got on pretty well. When he stood up reluctantly to leave, he invited me to his farm, and said what a nice afternoon he had had.

Imagination: The Gnomes and the Snake

The next patient, Ernest, was a large man with muscular arms and a checked woolen shirt. As soon as he came into the room he said, oddly enough:

"There's a snake on the floor".

I began to think that there was something infectious in my room. No, but I had inadvertently allowed a piece of string to fall onto the parquet floor. Although it lay there perfectly still, for Ernest it appeared to be moving like a snake. Therefore he spent the next few minutes carefully getting it out of the way under the table with his foot, before he could sit down and relax. We were then able to talk about the weather for a few minutes, before I dared pick up my "snake," so as not to upset things any further.

A few days later, Anna, a neatly-dressed grey-haired lady came in and shut the door quietly. She sat down meekly on the nearest chair, folded her hands on her lap and looked out of the window into the middle distance.

When I asked her why she was in hospital, she said: "My family said that I was cheating at cards".

She said that she used to play cards with the neighbors every morning, but one day all the cards were diamonds and the hearts were nowhere to be seen. She was therefore excluded from the card parties, and she said she had nowhere to go.

A month later, Anna was looking at herself in the mirror at home and asked: "Why is my niece in the room?". Her daughter told her that she was looking at herself, and this caused a row.

"I was right, you know," said my patient turning to look at me, "but nobody understood".

I thought that I would try to understand, and we could use the mirror in the consulting room. So I placed myself next to my patient and we both faced the mirror.

I asked her: "Who is that person standing next to you?"

Anna answered confidently: "That's one of those girls who works around here".

Since this was maybe not so far off from the fact, and since by then I realized that it was better not to disturb the sensory appreciation of my patient beyond a certain point, I let the matter rest.

We continued with the remainder of the examination and conversation. When we had finished, the ex-card player said that she would be pleased to come back and draw pictures and have a cup of coffee any time.

Al, Ernest and Anna, together with many other patients in the State Hospital, suffered from the effects of arterial disease of the brain, (cerebral athero-sclerosis), affecting their sense perceptions, so that they interpreted the world differently from the rest of society.

It is easy to understand that "ordinary" folks have difficulty in adjusting and putting up with sudden, often frightening, aberrations in other people's behavior. This is particularly so if they affect members of their own family, or people whom they have known for many years as "normal", and if the misinterpretations of the physical world endanger the patient.

Even when I and other neurologists can understand and explain how these fabrications from the surrounding world come about, we have trouble in keeping on the same wave-length as the patients. It is difficult to know how to accommodate all varieties of experience, let alone how to modify behavior so that society can carry on its affairs harmoniously and without too much dislocation.

How to step in and then step out of the world of "fantasy" that brain disease can bring about is not easy. Constant adjustment is required when trying to step into the other person's shoes. With the attempt, our feet hurt and continue to cause us distress. And we can never experience other people's experiences.

CHAPTER 16

The Person and the Persona

"Was that the doctor, Mum? She did not look like a doctor," said Jason, the small boy, in a high piercing voice.

I heard his question after I had walked out of the examination room and was writing my notes next door.

"Yes, that was the doctor Jason, but don't talk so loud."

Jason was a very bright six-year old who had come because of reading problems and disturbing the class.

He had whizzed through all the neurological physical examination with zest, and investigated the equipment in the room with happy curiosity. He wanted to know how things worked, and who was who.

That evening I attended a dinner in the local Country Club given in honor of a retiring colleague.

I sat opposite his wife whose taffeta dress rustled elegantly as she sat down and unfolded her napkin. We talked of her husband's many years of devotion to his patients and the hospital, and how hard it had been for her bringing up the four children with him rarely at home. After half an hour, she enquired:

"And what does your husband do? I have not seen you at the Club before but maybe you don't play golf?"

I answered, "No, I'm sorry I don't play golf. I am a colleague of your husband's and I do neurology; I am not married."

"Oh", she answered, "but you don't look like a doctor."

After that the conversation turned to the safer subject of her family vacations, since I felt that she was uncomfortable with a different image of doctors.

I did not think she wanted to explore the idea that a doctor stereotype may be unnecessary.

External appearances are not all-important. They cannot, however, be ignored, since we all have inbuilt images of certain roles in society, and when on the job doctors are not seeking to disturb people's preconceptions. "Kleiden machen leute." (Clothes make people). At other times, when not acting in a professional capacity, doctors are free to express their personal views of image, of persona, and the nature of work within societies.

How to be a person and a persona, a private individual and a public professional at one and the same time is tricky. I remain myself but I am receptive to outside interference and trying to identify with the patient. And with the next patient. And the next. And the next, as they come up the escalator, one behind the other.

What am I inside? What am I outside? Inside I must feel one. Outside I must look one. I am not different "on-duty" and "off-duty", but behavior must transcend personal emotions. Whatever internal turmoil may be going on, when "on-duty" I must be appropriately gracious, confident of what I know and knowing where to seek information when I do not have the expertise. Mood swings, with "highs and lows", are inappropriate behavior for the persona.

When patients first consult a doctor to tell their story, the one thing they want is to be listened to. The persona is a listener. As a listener my opinions are founded on knowledge but modified by experience. As experience increases, which means the older one gets, one should be able to present one's persona so that the patient feels comfortable. A skillful doctor has a flexible persona, so that he or she has a repertoire of styles, according to the patient's age and culture.

One hopes that the older doctor is therefore wiser than the younger; the good judgement of the older recommends procedures to the younger, who may be the more manually skilled operator. The older should be quicker in picking up clues, and better at linking association of factors so as to illuminate the case more clearly. If vested interests have not interfered with vision, complexities are more easily envisaged by those with experience.

If imagination has been retained, depth and breadth of perception should come easier with age. The persona adapts to varied situations.

Patients react to external appearances, to the persona.

Dickie aged nine had no speech, no smile and he dribbled whenever he walked up to the examination table; but his eyes always lit up when I wore my brightly-colored yellow silk dress.

Jenny, who sat rocking herself all day, would touch my skirt before she allowed me to come near her.

Hattie without speech was scared by anything new, but she was not afraid of my ophthalmoscope when she could play with my pendant made of glittering stones.

The children in this institution for the mentally retarded reacted to dress, color and the touch of fabric. Their reactions were more obvious than those of more socially inhibited "normal" adults.

Doctors may not take into sufficient consideration the reaction that outward appearance has on a first encounter. The young doctors are keen to get on with the job and may feel that appearance is trivial and not relevant. As I grew in experience, I admitted that these factors, which are part of persona, do have an effect.

Women have an advantage because they have greater scope for variety in outward appearance. They can probably alter the atmosphere of clinical medicine more easily than men by presenting different facets of their personality. The revolution in hospital and clinic atmosphere owes much to women who have contributed to interior decoration, and can alter the psychological climate of medicine. This may be because it seems easier for women to blend their professional persona with their private person.

Gender is relevant in some circumstances.

I was in charge of a clinical department, and worked closely with a male colleague who was in a more junior position. Many of the patients thought that the roles were reversed. The overall atmosphere of the department was enhanced by there being both a "mother" and a "father" figure for diagnosis and treatment, and this perception seemed valuable for the patients. The difference in our styles and personae provided variety which was professionally helpful.

During a first encounter, both the patient and the doctor are "on trial" and a doctor's persona is important. It can give confidence. When meeting a new patient, there are several factors causing the physician anxiety: shall I be able to make a diagnosis? If the diagnosis leads to serious disease, how can I mitigate the information so that the individual is not crushed right away? How do we start the investigations without causing unnecessary fear and anxiety?

Gender is an additional factor in this first encounter. Did the patient expect a woman doctor? and if so, does he or she have a preconceived idea of women doctors? In the early part of my career I did not consider this question. I just got on with the job. When I became more experienced, perhaps more sensitive to the patient as a person instead of as a "case", I was more aware of the potential effect of gender as part of persona.

Although first impressions can deceive, the initial encounter between patient and doctor is crucial. In non-emergency situations and particularly where attitude is all-important, the person of the doctor, as opposed to the persona, can play a significant part.

When the diagnosis indicates a trivial condition which the patient can adjust to and self-cure, it is important how I as the physician present this. How can he or she profit from the encounter? and feel that something useful has been learned. Will he or she run away from the psycho-physiological problem or look for serious disease, maybe unconsciously hoping for it? That individual may immediately seek another opinion, and compound the problem.

How do I present the obvious, or the obscure, the simple or the complex, the diagnosis that the patient expects, or fears, or wishes to carry back to the relatives? Every factor that applies to the patient also applies to the "significant others", the circle of friends, relatives, employers, workmates.

The clue is to lead up to the diagnosis as the patient tells his or her story so that the patient himself comes out with the words that indicate the diagnosis, even if the technical terms may differ. It is also important that, whenever possible, the interview is witnessed by a friend or family member, and that the diagnosis is written down and carried home by the patient. In this way, there is no conflict concerning what the patient said at the interview, and his/her memory is confirmed by the other person. In this way, the patient gains control over the situation and feels that he/she is a problem-solver.

I learned from experience always to ask the patient to invite the accompanying person to attend the consultation.

The choice lay with the patient. And the invitation reflected the person of the doctor rather than the persona.

Some diagnoses carry their special problems.

How is the doctor to present the diagnosis of epilepsy to the ambitious young man climbing up the professional ladder, or to the fiance who may be hesitant about the future?

Joan, a tall blonde aged 19, walked quietly into the consulting room behind her mother. Mrs. Bennet gave the history of Joan's epilepsy from early childhood, describing how carefully she and her husband had looked after Joan.

She had never been to stay overnight with friends; she had never learned to swim or to ride a bicycle, and she was usually accompanied by her mother if she went to a movie. Now Joan was offered a clerical job.

"So what do you recommend? Doctor. Is it safe for her to take the job?", Mrs. Bennet asked, leaning forward in her chair anxiously.

I encouraged Mrs. Bennet to describe her own fears, and the restrictions that she, Mrs. Bennet, had suffered. "If it were not so difficult for you, Joan, to get work," said Mrs. Bennet, "your father and I would have moved long ago out of this town to a nicer house."

Slowly Joan joined the conversation, and we agreed to investigate the epilepsy, do a brain-wave record, try various life-style changes and meet again.

Joan took the job, and over the years gradually made decisions gaining independence and adjusting the family dynamics.

Anxious parents of children with epilepsy often carry a load of fear, prejudice, resentment and guilt. The doctor needs to recognize their involvement, while at the same time to look after the patient's future. In such cases, the attitude of the physician is all-important, and this arises from the person rather than the persona.

I need to communicate my concern along with the realization that I am a buffer, a go-between, with the patient on the one hand and the condition, the disease and the reaction-to-disease on the other hand. The patient has to integrate his present self with the new information and knowledge and to fit it into his future which will often be different from the past. He or she is therefore required to change. And I become an instrument of change.

The challenge to doctors is how to present "change" as an exciting, worth-while goal. Few of us like change, and many of us resist it. It is not biologically acceptable; it requires an active state of mind, an act of the will.

Our fears of the unknown and our pre-conceived notions obstruct change; like sentries at a gate, they stand on the familiar pathway, asking the vital question: WHY CHANGE?

At this point, the doctor's attitude and personal values which make up the person as opposed to the persona, color the patient's decision-making. With a diagnosis that requires the patient to make active behavioral changes, the doctor can become more personal, presenting his/her more individual person. In order to understand and advise how the patient can best adapt to the diagnosis in the home and work environment, the personality of the doctor is called into play.

Sensitivity may be gained when a person has to adapt to illness, realizing that he or she is vulnerable and from that point of view, resembles the rest of humanity. There is an opportunity for the individual to gain through this adaptation rather than to lose. This sensitivity is excellently brought out in the book: "*When Doctors Are Patients*," (see bibliography), in which 33 doctors give their experiences during serious illness. Describing heart disease, Max Pinner, M.D. wrote:

"In the middle of the night,— I was travelling in a Pullman berth and woke up with a sudden sharp pain in my chest.— Recognition was instantaneous.— I knew that this was the beginning of a new epoch in my life."

Dr. Pinner went on to describe how: "I discovered that the prestige of my position had given some starch to the texture of my persona.— Now my life has regained a balance that it had lacked for years." He concluded that: "It is not the measure of joy and pleasure that matters, it is the intensity of living."

As the years go by, I am less afraid of showing my person, having I hope blended it with my persona. The emotions evinced by a medical situation are absorbed into the total experience of life, whether this is experience shared with friends, with family or with patients. The situations continue to demand different codes of behavior, but the underlying emotions aroused and transmitted are similar. For doctors the separation between the person and the persona gradually lessens.

Blending of person and persona becomes particularly important in a case when the patient's prognosis is bad.

It is easier when patients have successfully crossed the bridge of change and are "improving", because both patient and doctor enjoy this situation. The danger is that this enjoyment of "success" implies that "success" becomes equated with "getting well". We may then equate "not getting well", which is the natural course of many diseases, and death with "failure". Death is not seen as an inevitable part of living. This view-point plays straight into the hands of depressives.

In these situations, both the doctor's persona and person have an effect on the patient. The saying: "To leave is to die a little, and to die is to leave a little early" is true, but not easy to accept. It is difficult for physicians, as for patients, not to regard death as often a "failure". A "good job" done by both the doctor and the patient and family, prevents this sense of failure and does not let it add to already existing sorrow.

My persona may be wounded by the failure of a patient's death if my expectations were unrealistic and medically unsound. My person should remain relatively undisturbed, while I profit from growing with the intimate experience of life and death. I learn to be both professional and personal all in one.

CHAPTER 17

Compromise

I was passing through the Emergency Room on my way out to the car park. It was snowing and I was late for the orchestral concert of Guys and Dolls that I was playing in at Wisconsin Rapids High School. My violin was in the car.

"Doctor", said the Emergency Room nurse, "we have a case just come in; the child is unconscious."

The colleague who should have started on duty in the Emergency Room at that time was delayed upstairs with a difficult intubation, so I followed the nurse to examine the new admission.

The little girl who looked about three years old was lying on the stretcher, unresponsive to any stimuli and almost pulseless but without any obvious injury. The ambulance driver had been called urgently to the house by a neighbor who had heard cries, but we had no details of any kind. The driver had picked up the child at the door from the neighbor who did not wish to come in the ambulance.

After examination and recording the circumstances I made a provisional diagnosis of closed head injury, and telephoned the neurosurgeon, sharing with him my suspicions of unusual trauma. The unconscious child was taken upstairs for X-ray and emergency cerebral angiography. When the neurosurgeon crossed the threshold, I exchanged further information with him and went on out to the car.

As I rapidly brushed off the deep snow from the windscreen and drove off down the main street, I kept wondering: What were those cries? Who was in the house with the child? Why did the neighbor not come to the hospital?

I drove fast, too fast. The red light of a police car following me shone in my rear window, and I stopped for the familiar sound of a police car horn. The large policeman came lumbering slowly up to my driver's window. I picked up my convenient stethoscope from the seat and told him I had an emergency, not specifying whether in the past or the future. He was acquainted with our hospital, and I suppose that there was sufficient anxiety in my voice for him to overlook the speeding.

I arrived for the opening of Guys and Dolls, just as the conductor was in despair thinking that he had to start without his concert "master". I was his concert "master", and my stand partner was also agitated, thinking that she had to lead the orchestra in my place. Nevertheless, we started off only a little late and with determined attack. The teen-agers on the stage played their parts with gusto and the audience clapped exuberantly.

However, at the end of the performance the conductor, who was a mild and patient man, said to me rather mournfully: "Why is it that your violin playing is so variable and unreliable?".

It was difficult to explain to the conductor that I was distracted and felt torn in all directions. I was reliable as a doctor, and unreliable as a concert-master. People with amateur interests commonly try to do "too much". Compromise runs the danger of mediocrity.

Two months later the snow had melted and the trillium flowers were beginning to bloom in the Wisconsin woods. I was summoned to give expert witness regarding the medical condition of the child, who had died with complete occlusion of the carotid arteries on both sides of the neck. I drove 80 miles to the unfamiliar Court House, hoping I was not going to be late.

Awaiting our turn in the Court Room, I sat in a back room surrounded by shelves of law books bound in leather. I made stilted conversation with a woman in a black coat with pink hat and gloves, whom I discovered to be the maternal grandmother of my patient. Not long before the little girl's death, her father had returned from the Vietnam War, and her mother had disappeared. The milkman had heard the cries. The neighbor knew the milkman. I gave my medical evidence. There were no witnesses. Everyone in the small town knew the family, but nobody talked. I doubt that the case was ever fully "cleared up".

On the way back to hospital, I stopped to look at the white trillium blooming in the woods; I had never seen the flower before that Spring, but was to observe it in many later Springs. When I see it now, I think of the cries of a child that exasperate a disturbed parent; of the despair of mothers with unwanted pregnancies and unloved children; of the silences of communities; of the questions we dare not ask and of our inability to explain behavior.

I also realized that I was constantly compromising. One thing never seemed to get done "properly" because another event would interpose. The child's case history was perhaps hurried because my loyalty was half with Guys and Dolls. I played the violin out of tune because my mind wandered off to the mystery of the unconscious child.

With a variety of commitments each requiring loyalty, we may have to share out both the commitments and the loyalties, sacrificing one for another. Sharing out loyalty requires compromise which is not easy.

I compromise in my attitude to a patient, whether to evaluate him or her as a "whole" person or to focus more closely on their special problem in which I have expertise. The complexity of certain medical subjects requires differentiation into many sub-specialities. The patients may express frustration because subspecialists appear no longer to see them as "whole" people. We can be offering them the best service in that particular problem, but sometimes it may be wiser to leave a disorder incompletely diagnosed. The compromise for both patient and doctor is to accept imperfection.

A medically trained person who tends to be a perfectionist is better suited to the experimental laboratory, where variables can be better controlled than in ordinary life.

A medical practitioner needs to be content with ambiguity and compromise. Because more could always be done with patients, we compromise in our activities. We fail to read the latest medical literature every evening, and to attend the local political meetings which enhance community life. We neglect old friends and previous commitments when we give time and thought to our latest study asking, for example, why relapses occur in certain cases of multiple sclerosis and not in others. We compromise in our affections, when new colleagues offer opportunities which require us to change our environment.

Other types of compromise include the need to decide when and how vigorously to treat patients in certain circumstances.

I learned about this difficult quandary in Birmingham, England, from my "chief", a great neurologist. We were looking after a desperately ill patient, Hector, who was conscious but partially paralyzed from a brain tumor with a poor prognosis.

One night, Hector developed complications with swings in blood pressure, respiratory problems and increasing paralysis, but he remained conscious. Several of us struggled all night with maneuvers and procedures which overcame the crises.

The next morning, Hector was the first patient we visited. The tubes were in place, the records were neatly laid out, the patient was half awake, and the white bed cover was all tidied up.

Professor Johnson walked up to the bed with the head Nurse ("Sister") and the retinue of junior staff and students in white coats. I stood, bleary-eyed, at the head of the bed by Hector, who gave a wan smile to the assembled company. I recited the tale of the night's trials and tribulations.

Dr. Johnson turned to me with his usual kindly smile, and commented: "Triumph of technique over reason". He gave no further opinion, and I understood that our resuscitating efforts were perhaps misjudged. It had been a technical triumph; was it to be repeated next time? We all walked on to the next bed.

Was this a medical compromise, involving decisions concerning quality of life, and was this to be acceptance and compromise with the inevitable?

In later life, when I had the main responsibility of making ultimate decisions, each case was decided on its own merits and in its own context.

Compromises have to be made when it is unwise to offer technical medical advances to "all" people. This is a socio-economic issue administered at an impersonal level. A physician having a personal relationship with an individual patient makes similar compromises, but with a face attached to the regulations. Our loyalties are shared between the "well" public and the "sick". A hierarchy of values necessitates compromise. Individual sacrifices have to be made when larger issues for greater numbers of people are involved. Doctors may be accused of inconsistency when contradictory data cause changes in decision-making. It is not possible for regulations to fit every circumstance.

The price of tolerance is often ambiguity. Therefore dubiety with anxiety, as in the Birmingham case described above, are inevitable. The acceptance of grey areas in human affairs becomes part of the medical profession's armamentarium. Because we accept compromise in ordinary life, we also accept it in medical practice.

CHAPTER 18

Manipulators and Manipulatees

Cheryl came into the consulting room, a fragile-looking young woman with her head on one side.

She was a waitress who was beginning to bump into tables because her walking gait was unsteady. She upset the coffee into the laps of customers because of tremor of the hands. Her employer was saying to her that her speech was slurred, but Cheryl denied it.

Two years previously, she had lost vision temporarily, but she did nothing about it and it recovered spontaneously.

On examination, there was loss of sensation in the legs, and signs of abnormality within the central nervous system.

She was duly scared, but after appropriate tests and hearing that she was likely to improve within six to eight weeks, she recovered her spirits. She accepted treatment and took time off work, on advice, in order to rest successfully. Two months later, she returned to say that she felt fine.

Six months after this, Cheryl reported again that she felt well and was living with a boy friend. She brought me a present of a china bird sitting on a log, which I accepted with thanks for waiting room decoration.

A year later, Cheryl had a recurrence of unsteady walking and in addition a tight feeling as though she had a girdle around her waist. She had lost her job because her speech was slurred, and her bladder control was less good than before.

After repeated examination and tests that confirmed abnormality, I suggested that she should make an application to the Bureau of Social Services Disability

Insurance. The forms were duly completed by Cheryl and myself with the diagnosis of Multiple Sclerosis written in, and after an appropriate interval Cheryl received the regular payments.

Cheryl failed to show up for the next two or three follow-up appointments, despite our inviting letters and the telephone calls from our cheerful secretary.

One day the doorbell rang at home and a personal messenger from a law-firm delivered an official deposition that Cheryl was suing me because of a diagnosis of Multiple Sclerosis. A recent report from another neurologist stated that she now showed no abnormality.

On investigation by the lawyers of my medical coverage, it was found that Cheryl continued to draw Federal payments for this diagnosis.

During the next twelve months, paper files accumulated, with court appearances, charges of competence and incompetence, defenses of medical procedures, anxieties of newspaper reporting, hurt personal honor, inter-professional bad feeling and a rigmarole of wasted money, time and effort.

Finally the case was dismissed, categorized as "a nuisance case" by the Insurance companies. I presume that the Bureau of Social Services Disability Insurance continued to pay Cheryl, not knowing about upheaval at the local level.

I learned from this case the intricacies of manipulation.

I knew many patients with devastating chronic neurological diseases and admired them for their persistence in coming with a variety of requests to the consulting room, whether in August heat or January snow. They would ask for the latest treatment, or for a motorized wheel-chair, or a letter to their employer, or to fill up a form for a home help or other service. These patients were maneuvering appropriately and with courage.

The battle with disease involves the daily chores of coping, which means personal management or in other words manipulation of events.

The dictionary definition of manipulation is: (1) "to operate or control by skilled use of the hands," and (2) "to influence or manage shrewdly or deviously, especially for one's own advantage."

Shuffling activities shrewdly, rearranging the house with skillful advice from the occupational therapist, is necessary and appropriate manipulation. It may, however, lead to inappropriate manipulation of people at a later stage.

"Fate" can manipulate us, giving us a raw deal when we are hit by an alcoholic driver on the wrong side of the road, or by an allergic response to an unknown virus. We remain more healthily in control of the situation when we use our resources to manipulate our environment. This involves seeking out the doctors who will manage and manipulate on our behalf, using and influencing the Social Services, managing the "system" and the "theys" in society.

Over the years, I witnessed the ramifications of illness with different coping mechanisms. Some patients came with their fiancés to discuss the disease, and wanted their children to be praised for taking over duties such as cleaning and putting out the garbage cans. Some asked for statistics of progress, and wanted information from the national and international meetings I attended. These patients were appropriately making demands and manipulating their doctor in their own interest.

If we do not learn to manipulate our own wheel-chair around corners, to paddle our own canoe, and to lift the telephone when we want help, we shall rot in solitude. Every successful manipulatee (someone who is being manipulated) becomes a manipulator.

Doctors, by profession, are manipulators of bacteria, tumors, pain, pinched nerves, spinal cord compression causing paraplegia, and a thousand ills that afflict us. They are engaged in the battle that manipulates these ills. From this position, therefore, doctors are open to being manipulated by the owners of these bacteria, tumors, pinched nerves and other destructive forces.

Physicians and surgeons, therefore, have to distinguish between manipulation which benefits the individual affected without over-burdening others, and manipulation which becomes emotional blackmail. Because medical situations causing change have an emotional component, they may lead to a power-struggle between one individual and another, or within families, or between the life-forces that play upon those individuals. The goal remains the same: seeking to achieve and maintain control of the situation with a suitable amount of manipulation. This requires frequent readjustment because the circumstances are constantly changing.

Emotions of a Physician

The telephone rings, and a patient who has ruptured a congenital aneurysm is admitted in coma. The see-saw of the power structure is immediately clear. The doctor is in charge; the patient is the recipient, until further decisions are required. No one is being "manipulated" by another person; an outside force (a congenital fault in the muscle layer of one of the arteries in the brain) has caused the catastrophe.

However, once the emergency is over, and the patient, for example, has recovered from coma but is in a wheel-chair, he or she needs to take charge and manipulate the environment, including the doctor, so that the patients makes the best use of the opportunities. If at that point the doctor is unwise and encourages unrealistic goals, the doctor can be manipulated inappropriately by the patient and end up feeling frustrated and "used".

Manipulation can take many forms, and it may require several years of clinical practice to recognize them.

Mrs. Godlowski was a 42 year-old executive director of a prestigious firm engaged in the export trade. She came into the consulting room with a smile, and put her attache case down neatly by her side. She crossed her knees, and my eye instinctively went down to her elegant ankles in well-balanced high-heeled shoes. She told her story minutely, describing the episodes of unbearable migraine, when the throbbing pain would all but incapacitate her. Usually, however, she would just manage to get back home, collapse into bed, and close the curtains before terrible vomiting set in. Thereafter she was dead to the world for the next 48 hours, and her husband would have to do everything for her. This had been going on for 20 years.

I picked up the challenge eagerly. I prided myself as the one who could cure the headaches that had defeated previous doctors over so many years. I would understand the precipitating factors, and rescue both the patient and her husband from the bondage of these unpredictable headaches which threatened to destabilize the marriage.

Among other forms of treatment, we arranged that with the next crisis headache, I would immediately admit Mrs. Godlowski to hospital. When that day came, I interrupted what I was doing and dutifully met Mrs. Godlowski at the hospital door. She looked limp and fragile, and my heart went out to her. All the staff were primed to go into action: cold towels, warm bed, quiet room, quick injection, dim light, and monitoring equipment. When the crisis was over, quicker than usual, both doctor and patient felt encouraged.

Over the next few months, when Mrs. Godlowski called the tune, I responded; she was flattered at the attention, I was satisfied with my healing powers, and the patient's husband was pleased with his new freedom.

After about a year, when I was beginning to think that Mrs. Godlowski understood how to prevent the crises, and a new era of wellness was expected, the old pattern returned. I had an urgent telephone call and was bidden to the bedside immediately. When I arrived, Mrs. Godlowski greeted me with:

"My husband actually went out and played golf on this   very afternoon when I came home from the office with this terrible headache. As he shut the front door, he said: "You know what to do, Dora, remember what the doctor advised. I'll see you later. So what, Doctor, do you think of that?"

Emotions of a Physician

I did not say what I thought of that, but I was seriously rethinking my therapy and examining my failure in this case. I had failed medically, and I had not recognized potential manipulation. I had fallen into the role of the rescuer and had obtained only a stop-gap, temporary improvement, not a cure. I had allowed myself to be manipulated by the person and the situation. I was in much the same situation as the husband.

People who feel manipulated run the risk of feeling sorry for themselves. The evening of Mrs. Godlowski's crisis I sat alone by the fire and thought about illnesses and therapy in relation to the proverb: "Laugh and the world laughs with you; weep and you weep alone". Mrs. Godlowski felt deserted by her husband when she was suffering. I felt that my "best" efforts were not bearing fruit; I was unappreciated and manipulated.

As soon as I began to analyze the situation objectively without bias and without feeling sorry for myself, I developed a more effective plan of action. When that particular crisis was overcome, Mrs. Godlowski agreed to treatment by both a psychiatrist and myself the neurologist, approaching the disorder from different angles.

If one becomes a complainer, feeling manipulated by fate or one's family or workmate, people will steer clear of one's company and one will be left cheerlessly manipulating alone.

Doctor are trained to witness and listen to the sorrows of others. This does not mean, however, that they need to allow those who feel themselves manipulated to become manipulators in turn. Situations can remain free of manipulation.

Rebecca was an anthropologist who left London to complete a project in the Arizona desert. She knew that she had a brain tumor but guessed she had time for this last study. One day in Arizona she developed a severe headache from recurrence of the brain tumor. A friend telephoned to ask me for immediate action. Rebecca was admitted to hospital in Wisconsin and given intensive palliative treatment so that her son could fly with her back to London. Rebecca never complained. I was in tears as I said goodbye to her at the hospital door. I admired the heroism of acceptance.

The psychology of victims and victimizers is complex and related to manipulation. The concept of being in control of one's own fate is perhaps better understood by using the words "manipulatee" and "manipulator" than the words "victim" and "victimizer" which have a more passive/aggressive connotation. The challenge of health and illness is better confronted with as active an attitude as possible. For this reason, the motto of the mountaineer Dag Hammarskjold, Secretary General of the United Nations: "realization that fate is what you make it" is a wise inspiration. However, the outcome of some diseases is beyond one's control. Differentiating between what can be manipulated and what must be accepted is an art. In this respect, doctors are in the same position as patients, and we can learn together.

CHAPTER 19

Dependence and Independence, the Delicate Balance

I became acutely aware of my dependence on patients one evening when the snow covered the ground and muffled all sounds. The house was quiet; there was no fire in the grate; the books sat silently on the shelves. And I felt all jazzed up inside with anxiety.

How was that young man, Kevin, doing with his acute paralysis of Guillain-Barré polyradiculo-neuropathy? He had been admitted that morning with numbness and tingling, sensory loss and weakness of all four limbs. His respirations were all right that morning and his voice was strong and swallowing intact. But you never know. The paralysis can spread so fast that you need to watch very closely.

I had faith in the nursing staff and nobody had called me.

Why was I so restless? I went outside in the fast-falling snow, and shovelled the driveway to get the car out of the garage. I thought: "If I go now to see Kevin, I might feel less upset."

The wheels scrunched on the roads which were empty. But the doctors' car park was half-full, and it reassured me to know that many of my colleagues were in the hospital working.

I walked along the hospital corridor visualizing Kevin's chest wall going up and down. Was he as afraid as I was? Did he understand from all our attention that the paralysis might spread? Had we unduly scared him? Is anticipation worse than the event?

I spoke a few words to the nurse and drew up a chair at the bedside. All seemed as before, as he opened his eyes. The bedclothes rose and fell with the breathing. The nostrils did not dilate. The pulse was unchanged.

Dependence and Independence, the Delicate Balance

"How are you?" I asked.

"I'm fine, thank you," Kevin answered and closed his eyes again.

I held his hands; I tested the strength of the wrists, and I watched the slight movements of the limbs and the trunk as he turned over to one side.

I continued to feel the warmth of his hands, and I sat there some minutes longer. There was no change. No need for further worry. But there was contact. There was physical reassurance. There was contentment. The world turned right side up again. And my stomach stopped churning.

I smiled to the nurses, and walked back along the white corridors. The car was half covered in friendly snow. When I got home, I lit the fire and settled down to read a nice book. But that night I said to myself: "Just take that in. You are desperately dependent on patients, and that's more than it should be. Do something about it". I sat watching the blue flame curl; the log fell over and I understood how I was becoming over-dependent and must rectify the balance.

As doctors, we are dependent on our patients for the emotional support of being needed and welcomed; for our bread and butter; for motivation to continue discovering the oddities and wonders of human functioning; for ego satisfaction in achievement; for examples of heroism and baseness; and for a continuous stream of daily intrigue, gossip, and tales as gripping as those in the Arabian Nights.

For some physicians, the fundamental human factor underlying this dependence may be status and the boosting-up of the person as a pivotal member of a group, the reassurance of belonging to respected society, the feeling of doing good, or the label and a place of own's in the world.

I am what I am because I do what I do.

Most of us depend on a friend with whom to share our emotions. At the same time we appreciate the ability to do things on our own. Therefore, balance between dependence and independence on the see-saw of life is one of the fundamental ingredients for contentment.

To achieve this delicate balance is one of the most difficult things in inter-personal relationships. It is not, however, a subject discussed when a young person is choosing a profession.

A doctor-patient or patient-doctor partnership may not appear as a relationship with an emotional flavor. Yet many of the features in this relationship are similar to those in ordinary friendships. One significant difference is the transience in medical situations. There is a tacit understanding that the contact is to be temporary. However, at the beginning of an encounter, the duration of the relationship is usually not known.

How often we hear people say after the first visit to a new doctor: "You know, I really liked him."

Or: "I shan't go back there again. She didn't seem interested in me."

Less frequently, we hear remarks such as: "She got the diagnosis right away." Or: "He said that he didn't know what the answer was, but I know that he will look into it". Personal likes and dislikes still play an important part in choice of physician, even in this age of procedure-made diagnoses. Patients seem to wish to continue a relationship with a doctor based more on emotional support than on medical, so-called scientific skills.

Are we not, therefore, looking for a two-way flow of independence and dependence with the patient saying (or thinking) something like:

"You make the decisions, but give me the feeling that I am making them."

Or: "I will tell you what to do, and you tell me that that is the right thing."

Or: "Go right ahead and do the unpleasant thing which needs doing, but don't tell me about it."

There is also the dynamic aspect of the relationship. The ability to SHIFT one's attitude and strategy as time goes on is another ingredient in this dependence/independence balance for emotional well-being.

The basic elements of trust and support do not change with time. However, because we are dealing with evolving life (with birth and death being parts of the continuum of life), both doctor and patient face the inevitable need for CHANGE. Once a certain development has taken place, it is necessary to move on.

In many situations, the delicate balance of dependence and independence between partners is subject to change as time passes. The balance MUST change if the relationship is to remain satisfactory.

Dependence and independence are illustrated in team work, and the doctor-patient relationship can be likened to a team. As defined, individuals in a team share the same goal, the same problems, and the same information, but possess different skills.

However, the basic ingredients of a team relationship between patient and doctor may flounder on the fact that information, with technical knowledge and know-how, can never be completely shared. Nor is it realistically possible to have the same problems. There is a Native American motto: "I will walk a mile with you in your moccasins," which is philosophically nice but probably unobtainable. Nevertheless, with IMAGINATION the doctor can try to bridge the gap.

The patient wishes to be listened to and cared for with a personal touch. The doctor needs to be listened to and appreciated for experience and advice, even if disagreed with.

I learned the lesson of the dependence/independence balance between doctor and patient and between patient and family, while I was partaking in the life-drama of a great performer.

I had the privilege in London of treating and caring for Ruth over a decade of sorrows. She was a professional 'cellist, and one evening she and her husband were hosting a party. Near midnight Ruth suddenly fell unconscious on the sitting room floor with convulsions in a major epileptic seizure. The ambulance carried Ruth to hospital, and the guests took their leave in shock and sorrow.

A few days later, the neurosurgeon carried out a partial excision of a brain tumor, an unusual type of glioma. At that time, Ruth was at the height of her professional powers, a leader in the community and mother of three children. She and her husband were the heart and soul in many a gathering.

Dependence and Independence,
the Delicate Balance

After surgery, Ruth continued to practise her 'cello but now in her hospital bedroom, and the staff would congregate with pleasure. Radiotherapy never stopped her. She returned to her accustomed place in the orchestra. Slight facial asymmetry indicated to the "cognoscenti" that something amiss remained, but it blended into her radiant personality.

Odd events, however, came up as shadows in the blue sky, confirming the fears that her clear-headed husband harbored from the moment of the first seizure. Minor epileptic seizures persisted: incidents when she would suddenly stare blankly for a few seconds, or act inappropriately for a few minutes: she would put salt instead of sugar into a fruit dish, or stand stock still in the middle of the kitchen repeating: "What is —what is— what is?—". These episodes interrupted the feeling that all was well.

My heart sank every time as I watched, year after year, the pens of the electro-encephalogram (brain wave recording) print out large abnormal patterns on the paper. How was it possible for Ruth to be performing each week on the stage in the front row of the orchestra with this tumor still sitting in the brain?

Thus the fight went on. The neurosurgeon performed a second brain surgery. Ruth said to him:

"Please do not remove the part of the brain with which I play the 'cello".

She underwent another course of radiotherapy, and she then travelled the long road of one chemotherapeutic agent after the next. We met together in hospital for many hours, the team of surgeon, radiotherapist, chemotherapist and I the neurologist. The radio therapist and I would drop in to the home of Ruth and her husband to discuss our alternative policies and we would plan the next step. At one stage, I dreamt that Ruth was walking across a park, beckoning me across the grass and through the trees, and I was following her up the hill.

At first Ruth was an equal partner in the team discussing, monitoring and approving each step of treatment. But as her judgement and personality gradually faded away over the years, the decision-making fell more to her husband and the children who were becoming adult. She would sit and stare into space for hours, no longer smiling, but flat in mood and appearance, like the husk of a person, apparently devoid of feeling. In conversation, her replies (when they finally came after a long pause) were often irrelevant. And yet occasionally, when she seemed quite "out of it", she would interject a name, a memory, a fleeting thought that was very much to the point. These poignant moments increased the sadness of friends and family.

She became oblivious of daily needs, difficult to dress, unaware of her appearance, of urinary incontinence, or of a full bowel. The heroism of daily care, with every week becoming more physically unpleasant and emotionally wearing, shifted my role of loyalty to the family rather than to my patient. Bedpans and carrying-on daily life with the unresponsive shell of a previous wife is non-spectacular heroism.

With increasing disease, Ruth's independence dwindled to zero. When she lapsed into prolonged coma, she became just "the patient", like other dependent patients who keep doctors and family members tied to them by bonds of duty. The family's emotional involvement changed. Their affection was reversed and turned toward distaste, so that their dependence/independence balance was in danger of upsetting. The doctor's dependence on the reward of personal attachment diminished. But my independent medical professional responsibilities increased, because I was left more alone. I had to continue my job, but without the support of the family.

The challenge in medical practice is for doctors to build up and maintain their own inspiration, in part independent of the patients.

The patient is dependent on the doctor's skills. In addition, he/she also demands and to a certain extent feels dependent on the doctor's empathy. At the same time, the patient needs to maintain or regain independence as an individual, with a "persona", a place in society and in his or her own family circle.

Hattie was a black lady from Alabama who had come North in her twenties to work ina tanning factory. At the age of 60, whe had a severe right-sided stroke, and spent six weeks in the Rehabilitation hospital learning to become independent again. She lost her speech with the stroke but she still managed to smile, and when she began to get words back she said to me:

"My chickens are waiting for me. I want my chickens." So her daughter took her back to the South.

A year later Hattie came walking into the doctor's office with a cane and a photograph of white chickens pecking outside her front door. It was as though Hattie were saying:

"Give ME the credit for all the hard work you put me through," and I did.

Emotions of a Physician

In situations such as these, a mutual admiration club is established. Both of us felt good about ourselves. At the beginning we are mutually dependent on each other. When the patient goes away he/she regains his independence. Probably more often than not, he/she forgets the doctor.

The doctor, however, speaking for myself, has a lingering feeling that she continues to need recognition for skills that can only be appreciated by her peers, those who understand the intellectual problems involved. The praise of colleagues and the distribution of medical honors serve this purpose.

All patients have to "abandon" their doctor, but the doctor keeps a concerned memory for the "cases". This is an investment of emotion for the subject stripped of the individuals who were the vehicle for her interest.

At the appropriate moment, the doctor needs to "release" patients from the bondage of dependence.

"No, Mrs. Jones, you don't need to come and see me again. Your headache has gone. Throw the pills away. You know all that is necessary to know about your condition."

The patient leaves, but the doctor's emotional investment remains; the long-term investment of emotion in people who have headaches.

Our emotional well-being depends upon keeping the delicate balance of dependence and independence stable.

CHAPTER 20

Justice should be done, and justice should be perceived to be done

The front doorbell rang, and I left the stove where I was cooking for a dinner party.

The postman handed me a special delivery legal-sized envelope, and I signed the registered mail form. The guests were due, and I went on with the cooking.

Before going to bed I opened the envelope. I read that an ex-patient who had been treated at one internationally known institution was suing another institution of equal standing, and that I together with a friend and ex-colleague were involved on opposite sides in a quarter of a million dollars law suit.

I had worked at both of these named institutions, and the patient in question had been treated at both places at an interval of time.

When the lawsuit was announced, I had recently married.

I had faith that the lawsuit (my first) would be settled out of court, but still I knew that the sight of a quarter of a million dollars claimed, although only on paper, would disturb my husband, unused to the annoying stresses of medical practice. Within the next two years, he became our office manager and in control of all the peccadilloes of medical life. Meantime, I did what lawyers tell me doctors are in the habit of doing; I did not share that lawsuit anxiety with my spouse until later.

As predicted, the lawsuit was settled out of court, after honor, judgement and erudition had been put to the test; and after a considerable amount of professional time had been expended.

Emotions of a Physician

From the doctor's point of view, the main determinant of emotional disturbance in cases of medical malpractice is attitude, and this arises from long-standing self-esteem and tolerance of the view-point of others. In the situation just described, my self-esteem was not altered, because my medical behavior was no different in that case from many others. During the time that the patient was under my care, our relationship was pleasant and friendly. I tolerated the fact that she had a change of mind when she decided to sue, because presumably she did not appreciate that technical advances had altered diagnosis and treatment in the period between our relationship and her suing. Although justice was done in the first place, it was not perceived at a later date as being done.

Along with colleagues in similar situations, I continued to sign my name on 30 or 40 documents per day, usually without the time to read them over, and to go about medical business as usual. However, it must be admitted, maybe not as blithely as before.

This is not the place to discuss the changing scene of medico-legal politics. The story, however, illustrates the deeper relationship that exists between doctor and patient. Doctors are attracted to the field of medicine for varied reasons, without consideration of legal issues. They may become tied to the profession, even addicted, in their search for information into human nature. The nature of the link pulling doctors towards people in this particular context may in some cases be altered by the emotional overtones of episodes of suing between the parties. How do we as doctors react to this tie? this link? What kind of psychological defense do we employ in this field? Is it possible that what used to be considered a life-time of "saving the injured" may become a defensive fight in which emotions blur the issues?

The second case described below, with an account of the emotions aroused, may provide some insight and partial answers to these questions.

I treated a man aged 72 for epileptic seizures which had developed with a stroke and cardiac arrest following surgical removal of cancer of the rectum. His convalescence was stormy with evidence of brain damage, and he was treated with several medications along with physical therapy and other attempts at rehabilitation. Two or three weeks after surgery, his wife and daughter requested that I should reduce the medication being given to prevent the seizures because they believed that he was "over-drugged" and too sedated. We discussed the risks of medication reduction. I agreed to their request. Shortly after, the patient had a further seizure. His general condition continued to deteriorate and he was later admitted to a nursing home, where he died three years later of cancer with metastases in the lung.

Four years after I had treated the patient in hospital, I stood in the witness box. The patient's wife and daughter sat staring straight ahead with their backs against the uncomfortable wooden seats.

"What did you say to the family, Doctor, on that morning of April 16th?"

"When they asked me to reduce the medication, I discussed the. risks with them and said we will think about it."

It so happened that I remembered the conversation pretty well, because I had flown back across the Atlantic on the previous night, returning from my sister's funeral.

For seventeen days we listened to lawyers artfully manipulating witnesses, and I studied the faces of the jury with interest. We watched the lawyers huddle in hallways and recess behind closed doors while we stood around in the court room making meaningless conversation. At the end of the seventeen days, a financial settlement was made between the insurance companies. The family presumably received monetary "compensation" for grief. Was their anger appeased? Did they believe, as I did, that they were displacing their frustration of those years onto the doctors and hospitals? that they instigated the suit because of displacement of anger at the entire situation?

What emotions did I go through in court? I felt that my honor and my competence were attacked. I was scared that I and my colleagues might have local publicity, and be misunderstood. By good luck, there was no publicity and no misunderstanding, so that fear dissolved. As for competence I knew that I had acted legitimately. The fact that I had complied with the wishes of the family in a way that was medically acceptable was ironic, and an example of the vagaries of human behavior. My emotions were further dispelled when my lawyer explained to me that the doctors' insurance companies prefer that doctors go to jury trial when they believe that the case will be won, because it will cost them less. I still harbored resentment at my honor being questioned. But once I accepted that the action of the relatives was inappropriate displacement of their anger, I rid myself of that emotion. I am, however, left with sadness that the relationship between doctors and patients can be clouded by issues such as these. Justice was not perceived as being done.

In the interaction between the doctor and the patient, each partner in the contract or the transient relationship requires to feel that "justice" is done. By "justice" is meant the best solution and outcome in any particular situation. That situation may carry greater or lesser risks of a "good" or "bad" outcome; a situation in which either good health or death may be the outcome.

The doctor-patient interaction depends in part on the pre-existing outlook that each one brings to the situation. The outlook, in turn, is influenced by the attitude, personality and psychological state of each of the individuals.

Doctors, like other people, are unlikely to have taken the time and the opportunity to think out their outlook on life, before they plunge into these complex relationships with patients.

Physicians and surgeons in training and early professional life have a set of goals: to pass exams, to find a job, to finance a working situation, to harness enthusiasms, to cultivate good working habits, and probably to establish a family and a home. To examine one's own psyche is not usually part of a go-getter's program. There is not an immediate reward for introspection. The patients desire instant gratification. The doctor has similar feelings, plus the immediate need to satisfy the patient's needs. We can all be likened either to a young bird sitting in the nest with open mouth waiting for food to fall into the squeaking hole, or to a parent bird flying back and forth in a frenetic dash to keep up with feeding time.

We perceive justice to be done when we think that we ourselves have been justly done by. As a doctor, our reaction to being criticized which may lead to being sued for malpractice is influenced by our attitude to other people's problems and other people's thinking. In many cases, we can understand that a patient's frustration with a situation leads to displacement onto an accessible object, in this case the doctor. The patient could not perceive justice as having been done because he or she appeared to be unjustly victimized by the whole situation.

Issues such as justice do not seem to arise in day-to-day activities. Doctors, however, need to take time to understand what they are doing psychologically to and for themselves in their relationship with patients. They need to feel good about what they are doing with patients and about what they are saying to patients. The first is often a good deal easier than the second. This is because what to DO in a particular medical case can on the whole be written down and learned out of a book. For this or that infection, you should give this or that antibiotic. For such and such cancer, it is appropriate for you to excise or irradiate or target the appropriate organ.

The spoken word, however, what a doctor should or could say in any particular medical case, also needs to be appropriate, but can never be written down in a book because it is so variable. It depends upon the context. It depends upon the individual patient or relative with whom the doctor is talking. It takes both imagination and learning from experience to perceive "where the other person is coming from"; what their psychological needs are; and their educational background; and the reason why the patient consults the doctor at that particular moment.

These are tedious considerations for an activist, a doer who wants to "get on with it". They are also inappropriate in many medical situations, including emergency cases. Who wants a doctor to enquire about a patient's psychological needs when there are only four minutes in which to save a brain from brain-death following an auto accident? Who stops to ask "where are you coming from?" when a 30 year-old lawyer comes into the Emergency Room with acute obstruction of his heart coronary arteries? Who asks a teen-ager how he gets on with his parents when his appendix is nearly bursting?

In many cases, not only emergency ones, but more routine ones, such as common infections, injuries causing pain, headache without significant abnormality, and a wide range of disorders, doctors may DO the right thing and yet "justice" is not perceived as being done. This difference in perception is inherent in all human relationships.

We employ the phrase that is in our make-up, in our belief-system. Our vocabulary comes from our background. "Bedside manner" has in the minds of many of us become synonymous with personal charm and a degree of hypocrisy. Doctors may tell the patients what they wish to hear, and this may or may not be appropriate. When faced with tragedy, many people can be helped by feeling that they are at "the eye of the storm". They arouse attention and can derive comfort from everybody "gathering round".

"Justice" may be perceived to be done in the short run, but not in the long run. On-going experiences can cloud past events, and on-going disease changes attitudes.

In some circumstances it is not easy or even possible for doctors and patients to have the same conception of justice. The emotional climate, however, will be improved when all parties tolerate the differences in opinion without feeling personally injured.

In the best circumstances, the relationship ends once the problem is "resolved" to the satisfaction of both parties. However, in diseases such as cancer, diabetes, multiple sclerosis, strokes and hardening of the arteries in the brain, AIDS and many others, the relationship continues indefinitely. If doctors and patients see themselves as partners fighting disease alongside each other, there is little risk of antagonism.

If, however, they perceive themselves as being on opposite sides of a fence, misconceptions are likely to arise. Whether or not justice is done, it is the perception of injustice that leads people to sue. Although no two people can think alike, perception of justice needs to be approximately similar in the minds of all the participants.

CHAPTER 21

Good Advice Which Cannot be Taken

Keith was an attractive young man aged 22 with epilepsy following a motor accident causing a severe head injury. The neurosurgeon who referred Keith to me had operated successfully saving his life. The "only" problems that remained were seizures which required prevention and unemployment which required retraining. These, however, proved to be considerable problems.

After Keith's initial examination and electro-encephalogram (brain wave) recording, I recommended medication which was to be monitored according to his feelings of well-being and the blood levels. I reviewed with him precipitating causes of seizures, including alcohol abuse. Then I proposed a plan of action for the future with which Keith agreed.

We arranged for Keith and his fiancée to come for consultation. They would then have the opportunity to ask questions, to relieve anxieties or misapprehensions and to give themselves hope and a realistic appraisal of the situation. Keith was to hear about his medication level which had been inadequate because of not taking the prescribed drug. He was also to learn about the Office of Transportation regulations to prevent him and his family getting disturbed about the driving licence. All these consultations would be paid for by his insurance.

Keith and his family were also invited to attend free seminars which I gave every month in which participants discussed seizure prevention; the subject for the next seminar was employment for people with epilepsy.

Keith missed the first appointment, and we sent him a reminder and another appointment.

Two weeks later the telephone rang at 6 AM on a Monday when I had a full day's work planned. The nurse in a far-away hospital Emergency Room told me that Keith was being admitted with epilepsy, and would I please come and see him right away. When I got there, I found that seizures had occurred after a weekend of alcohol abuse, and that he had smashed his car on a lamp post.

After that particular crisis, when Keith had been discharged from hospital, we started over again in the hope of improved motivation, with explanation, education, medication, and battling employment problems.

For some months, things were better, his epilepsy was controlled and he got employed in a warehouse. A year after the initial head injury, the future seemed to be opening up. Then sadly, Keith returned to alcohol drinking, and his seizures recurred. He lost his job and his fiancée. He repeatedly failed to turn up for appointments, and did not answer letters or telephone calls to his family. Presumably he slipped into depression and the great unseen back streets of urban misery.

Why could the good advice not be taken? Maybe our program for rehabilitation after the head injury, looking simple to me, was too far removed from his behavior prior to the head injury. He had insufficient family support. Maybe his self-esteem was lower, and his temptation to alcohol stronger than I realized. Lacking staying power, Keith had failed himself, and I had failed to get my message accepted.

Good Advice Which Cannot be Taken

Mildred was a middle-aged, overweight lady who worked in a laundry. She thought that she was in good health, until she woke up one morning in August with partial paralysis of the left arm and leg. I met her frustrated to be admitted to hospital in a wheel chair, unable to walk. She was further upset when hypertension and diabetes were also discovered, having contributed to the stroke. My colleague started treatment for the diabetes.

After rehabilitation, Mildred returned to work at the laundry. We advised her to come for regular neurological checkups, and to attend evening classes at the local hospital for education on diabetes, diet, and stroke prevention. She never turned-up. She never answered the telephone calls, and I was anxious when "NO SHOW" was written on her chart several times after missed appointments.

Four months passed. Then one December morning at two o'clock the telephone rang: Mildred was being seen in the Emergency room in the local hospital with another stroke. She was in near-coma, and her diabetes was out of control. The family was all upset, and the new young Emergency doctor wondered why my colleague and I were not looking after our patients properly.

Why could the good advice not be taken? Maybe Mildred denied the seriousness of her condition and the warning given by a minor stroke that she needed to keep her blood pressure and diabetes under control. Maybe she said to herself: "Why me?" and felt that being a patient was an indignity? Was it fear, procrastination and resentment at having to take advice? A perceived loss of independence? As a disregarded adviser, I felt inadequate and defeated. I also had to resist feeling resentful.

Emotions of a Physician

Carl was a prosperous business man who first consulted me on account of pain radiating down the arm, which his friends suggested might be due to a "pinched nerve". I recorded hypertension and the electro-cardiogram indicated myocardial ischemia, (the heart muscle being short of blood). I referred him to a cardiologist who advised anti-hypertensive medication, and changes in his diet and life-style. He attended the first session in which these changes were discussed, but stated that he knew all about them and anyway was too busy to follow-up.

Three months later, we heard that Carl was being admitted with an acute myocardial infarction (heart attack) and probable stroke at another hospital, and that another cardiologist and neurologist were looking after him.

The frustration of giving the "right" advice and of having it rejected outright is hard to conceive by those who have not had this experience. This rejection happens to doctors over and over again, and we are totally unprepared by our medical training to accept this experience.

In these cases, our attitude as a doctor must not change. As Rudyard Kipling might have said: our enthusiasm must not flag; our smile must be as spontaneous as before; our step as light; our intonation as up-beat. But we are not all as heroic as that.

Examples such as those just given occur in probably every sphere of medical treatment: post-traumatic syndromes; chronic pain; gastro-intestinal disorders; drug abuse ("substance abuse"); many auto accidents and their sequels; anxiety attacks; headaches; domestic crises of various hues; and many more potentially preventable conditions.

When patients act contrary to advice the behavior is considered to represent "non-compliance" or more correctly "non-adherence".

The reasons for someone not listening to advice are of course legion, and this is not the place to analyze these complex factors. The effects on the physicians who recommend a course of action which is ignored are also complex. They may deal partially with their frustration by describing the patient as "non-compliant". But a doctor's internal frustration at being defeated does not go away by giving a situation a label.

The gnawing anxiety persists: why was my excellent advice ignored? Why was I ineffective and not listened to? Did I not make myself clear? Why did I fail?

No one likes being a failure. Even if we can say: "It was the other person's problem", we feel that it is OUR job to know how to treat people with diseases or how to get them to treat themselves. That emotion may indicate a need for control bordering on omnipotence. But it still motivates one to keep trying.

We therefore turn to books on "communication". We employ assistants, smiling people who may communicate our good advice effectively with patients; but meanwhile we feel a failure. Our logic tells us that we should only feel a "partial" failure; but still it nags inside. And our muscles tighten up; our fatigue grows; our coronary artery disease increases; and we lose our joy in the practice of medicine. "Time to quit" we say, as we swallow a whiskey and soda.

Emotions of a Physician

It was not the fault of the medical school, or of our professors who were busy teaching us the biochemical pathways for the metabolism of carbohydrates, and did not have time allotted to give us the technique for motivating diabetics to avoid the complications of diabetes. The people teaching metabolic pathways were not experts in human psychology.

As a medical student, eager and starry-eyed, I would rush off every Saturday morning to attend diabetic clinics and examine the people with peripheral neuropathy, complications of diabetes. At that time I never understood that complications were largely preventable if the patients had learned about the disease and were conscientious about themselves. I just thought that it was my job to identify the abnormalities, and classify the complications.

The patients who turned up at the clinics were the men and women who adhered to the program. We never talked about those who did NOT appear, those who ignored appointments and were much more at risk than those who attended. In addition, those who did come could have learned that it was probably the small intake of alcohol which when added to their diabetes gave them diabetic neuropathy.

I have learned to be far more concerned about the patients with epilepsy who do NOT keep their appointments or give a reason for disappearing, than the ones who come faithfully. The patients who do not surface, except in Emergency hospitals where they cannot be given long-term care, lead very sad lives.

Can we improve our communication of good advice?

In the medical profession we often lack ordinary imagination and common sense, not erudition and conscientious, hard-working habits. Can we "accuse" people of lacking in imagination when it is an indefinable quality? What yardstick measures imagination? Who defines the fluid boundary between "flakiness" and imagination? Can we reproach the conscientious, the zealous, the loyal, the dependable, the industrious, the stalwart, the upright?

No one person can be all things to all people, and we recognize our different roles and varied skills. However, good advice gets across more easily with a grain of imagination.

One morning I was attending an out-patient clinic at a specialized hospital for neurological diseases, a center internationally recognized for excellence. A Canadian colleague sat on one side and an American on the other.

A middle-aged, well-dressed woman was trying to give her history to the neurologist. She had pain, and he asked her all the appropriate questions in the logical order so that we could learn our "trade". But she never got her story across: she was discursive, while he was logical.

"Good morning, Mrs. Harris, and what are you complaining of ?"

"My arm hurts all the time".

"What kind of pain do you have?"

"I can't sleep, I have to get up and walk around the house all night and when —"

"Where do you feel the pain?".

"I've tried every kind of pill, and they only make me sick so then I —

"How long have you had this pain?"

"I keep telling you, I can't even use the vacuum cleaner it hurts so much so then I had to —"

"Do you have any numbness?"

"It feels like an electric shock when I touch that spot, and I think —"

"Which spot?"

"So my husband tells me I've become such a bore that life is —".

"Mrs. Harris, I asked which spot you were meaning?"

"I told him last night we can't go on like this, with me not able to open a can of soup or —"

"Do you have any weakness?"

"I can't even do my hair in the mornings because when—"

"We were not talking about doing your hair, Mrs. Harris, we were talking about the pain".

"But that's what I mean, doctor, nobody understands when I —"

"I think that we had better go on to the examination now".

After a prolonged examination which caused more pain, the neurologist gave appropriate advice. Mrs. Harris, however, was adjusting her hair and her scarf, and I could see that she was not listening.

"I'll write to your doctor", said the neurologist, attempting to smile. Mrs. Harris left without anything written down for her. I visualized her arriving home and the husband asking: "What did the neurologist say, Margaret?"

"I don't know," Mrs. Harris would answer, " he didn't say anything; he just poked and prodded, and didn't listen to me."

In the meantime, when the patient had left the room, the neurologist gave us a long erudite differential diagnosis and analysis of the syndrome.

Mrs. Harris had not answered the doctor's questions and yet she was giving him all the information although in a different format and in a different order from what he wanted. She told her story in the intervals between his questions, which interrupted her tale, and he gave her advice while her mind was attending to her own concerns.

The lack of meeting of the minds hit me forcibly that morning. I sat on the bench, reverential in front of the depth of the neurologist's knowledge and admiring his questing mind and the scanning process of diagnosis, but suffering acutely as I identified with that woman. Maybe she did not notice the gulf between the two of them; maybe she did not suffer; but maybe she was deeply wounded; maybe she still remembers the encounter to this day, as I do.

I resolved that morning that I would try at least on some occasions, maybe on most, to let the patient's flow of thought go uninterrupted until I had picked up a large assembly of clues. We all know that this is what the psychiatrists are trained to do. But doctors with a waiting room full of patients are not always in a position to allow patients the luxury of free thought association, particularly at the first encounter.

The skill of giving QUALITY time is not synonymous with QUANTITY of time. A session in which both patient and doctor ramble is often inappropriate. One effective word, one meaningful smile can replace the logorrhoea of a monologue preaching doctor.

Dogma is a dry diet, and nothing can replace flexibility with imagination for fallible people.

Good advice can sometimes be taken.

CHAPTER 22

The Parade: Can Doctors be all Things to all People?

Everyone loves a parade, particularly young people, eager to see the world. We run to the window when we hear the drums at the far end of town, we call to each other and watch the flags go by, waving in the wind. Round the corner come the marching trumpeters, the player with the big drum hanging round his waist, the trombones catching the sunlight as they telescope in and out, the giant tuba bringing up the rear. We love the young women twirling batons, the cart covered in flowers, the smiling faces and the flaring skirts, the elephant patiently plodding with dignity as if in a far-away forest, and the painted cart with the announcements calling us to come and see the circus in the fair ground.

The life of medicine brings with it a parade, the parade of people of different ages, races, backgrounds and needs. Not only do we watch the parade, but we partake in it. We are carried along in the streets, disguised maybe like a clown, reacting to the crowd. We often have to cover our faces with white powder, or hide behind masks.

We are supposed to be "all things to all people", although of course we know that that is impossible. Even knowing this, I was surprised to learn of the wide divergence of the patients' impressions of my professional self.

I carried out a survey by questionnaire of 500 patients whom I had treated for chronic headache over a 5-year period. I had examined them as out-patients under the same circumstances, and given treatment. They were diagnosed as suffering from migraine or muscle tension headache or post-traumatic headache following an accident, or a mixture of these problems.

Emotions of a Physician

There was an 85% response to this written questionnaire. The answers tabulated statistically showed on the whole good improvement, (attributable to a number of factors including the simple passage of time). What particularly surprised me, however, were the written comments which I had invited. To these patients, I appeared as a devil or an angel, as a cold uncaring monster or as a warm-hearted understanding doctor. I had to agree with a neurosurgical colleague who said to me one day when I was feeling a failure:

"Don't worry, you can't win them all".

We cannot be all things to all people.

There are several reasons why patients react differently to a particular doctor, even if that doctor is concentrating on one disease or symptom, for example chronic headache, and therefore has a fairly uniform approach to the subject. First of all the doctor may be either full of energy or tired on a particular occasion. The interview may take place early in the day, or after ten other patients have all complained of headache for the past five, ten or twenty years. Clearly one should not try to treat a chronic condition when fatigued, but appointments must be kept.

More significantly, however, the variable response is probably related to the doctor's ability to relate. Communication has many aspects. I was always interested in the symptom headache, but how much interest did I convey to the person with the headache? We are not all things to the needs of all people, although our energy is invested in the disease-process. Our passionate desire to conquer the disease is not synonymous with an emotional desire to be "all things to all people".

The Parade: All Things to All People?

The life of a medical practitioner requires adjustment to a parade, the parade of people with their individual reactions to the "same" diseases. It also requires an understanding of the context of the patients presenting with this "same" disease. Do we see the rows of anxious faces sitting in the waiting rooms of noisy hospitals as a parade of people with disease problems, or with problems brought about by their context, their physical and social environment?

Are we to be onlookers or participants in society? Are we simply to listen to the complaint of the pain in the back, or are we to help modify working conditions and reduce back pains? Is it only the complaint and the "Why me?" of the patient that we attend to, or do we in addition seek to ameliorate the context of the tragedy?

When I as a doctor open my eyes to the scenes of slums as I drive through the streets morning and evening on my way to and from hospital, do I divorce the head injury with the broken bottle from the fight at the street corner? Can I face this parade of anger and tragedy without building up my internal resistance to these scenes?

It was my job in a city with major problems to study the cause of acute strokes, and to quantify the amount of oxygen required by the brain with strokes. Every day I drew blood from the jugular bulb draining the brain, (the "bulb" is at the junction of the head and the neck), and we examined the contents of the blood to study the pathological events. Many of the patients were unconscious. The name on the wrist of many patients was "John Doe". After a time I asked my technologist Joan:

Emotions of a Physician

"Why are so many Americans called John Doe?" Joan answered: "Because when they are brought into the Emergency Room by the police, they or their relatives are afraid to give their name and address."

In this city, while caring for the unconscious patients, I had difficulty in ignoring the social situation.

Physicians are not social reformers or politicians. And yet we are part of suffering society. Society, the lawyers, the sociologists and the patients probably find us more responsive to their needs if we are in touch with the world in which we function.

It is easier to relate to individuals than to the "great anonymous crowd". The most surprising situations can be understood when the individual is known. I am equipped to respond to the social factors in any particular society as they affect an individual.

For many years, I treated a polite young married man, Harvey, for seizures. He always kept his appointments punctually, and he would sit with his bald head bent over the Bible in the waiting room. Although Harvey was rejected for many jobs because of epilepsy, he seemed to accept the situation when we worked together for his better employment. He supplemented his poorly paid job sweeping the city streets by working nights in his father-in-law's Funeral Parlor. He gave his spare time to canvass for the local school board candidate. Harvey seemed to be doing well from the epilepsy point of view.

One day his devoted wife called me up in great distress. Her husband had robbed the bank in an armed hold-up over the weekend, and was having continuous seizures in the county jail. The bank robbery had apparently been a well-planned affair, and not associated with "black-outs" of epilepsy. Because the police did not have the necessary pills and medication was suddenly stopped, severe seizures had started. I was startled, reconciling the picture of a well-behaved Harvey with an armed bank robbery.

I struggled through complicated and time-consuming intervention with various authorities. First, Harvey got back his pills. Then I wrote letters of explanation to lawyers, and a rigmarole of consequences followed. Fortunately, I was familiar with both Harvey's background and the local city scene.

After this episode, Harvey returned for his regular visits to neurology, the Bible was again in the waiting room, and the search for a better job was resumed.

Two years later, Harvey obtained a clerical appointment in the Department of Statistics at the Medical School. The long struggle paid off; the seizures were better controlled; he was integrated back into society, and his spouse was happy.

For Harvey, my role was more involved than simply that of a neurologist.

In other cases, detective work is required.

Peter, a tall boy aged 17, was driving home from skiing with his friends one Saturday night in December. The roads were icy, and the party was cheerful with alcohol when the car skidded into a tree. Peter was admitted to hospital in coma with a head injury. Two months later, he was walking around and had regained use of his arms. However, he suffered from "agnosia", a loss of knowledge of the nature of objects so that he could not distinguish between edible and non-edible material.

At the Convalescent Home, Peter and the nurses played draughts together. The nurses became fond of Peter because he told them funny stories, and was apparently less worried by his disabilities than were his doctors.

I began to get reports that Peter was having difficulty in swallowing. At first I thought this was due to a transient sore throat, but it became obvious that Peter was beginning to gag and even turning away from food, which was very unlike him.

One February night in a blizzard, the nurses telephoned to say that Peter could not swallow anything and what were they to do? I arranged for Peter to be transferred back to the acute hospital. The surgeon's car got stuck in the snow, but fortunately I lived near enough to the hospital to travel on cross-country skis and I met the radiologist in the X-ray room. Nothing could be seen in Peter's throat on careful X-ray screening.

I then described everything that Peter did in the Convalescent Home. Later that night two surgeons had what they called a fishing expedition, and by skillful placing of a flexible tube down Peter's esophagus (gullet) under anesthesia, they pulled up a plastic checker (draught).

No one in the Convalescent home had played checkers (draughts) since Peter's last game or remembered to count the number of checkers. Next day Peter returned to the Convalescent Home, and we all breathed a sigh of relief.

The Parade: All Things to All People?

Patients can expect their doctors to detect hidden disease factors as part of working with a mixed parade.

In some cases, physicians are merely spectators, but have the privilege of learning about the unusual activities of their patients.

One day in July an attractive blonde woman, Julie, in a cotton dress walked into the consulting room because of pain in the wrist from a fracture. The bone had healed fairly well, but baking bread was painful. Every day she rose at dawn to bake for the nuns in the convent. She had been born on a farm and joined the Franciscan order at the age of 19. She was now 35.

Three months before, at Eastertime, she had had a dream of flying over the cornfields of the family farm and touching the clouds. With a passionate desire to fly she joined a sky-diving club and learned to sky-dive. It caused her exquisite pleasure throughout May and June.

One Saturday shortly before sunset, she thought she was near her family farm and in excitement took a dive. Miscalculation landed her on the hard highway with a fractured wrist. However, the experience was reward for Julie, and even the resulting pain was of less importance to her than the sky-dive. I arranged that she should be off bread-baking duty.

With treatment Julie's wrist pain disappeared and she returned to baking at dawn and diving at sunset.

Day after day, the parade goes by, and the unexpected turns up. The world for the medical professional is full of adventure. Doctors can only be "some things to some people". On the other hand, many people can bring many facets of living to their doctors.

CHAPTER 23

Addiction to Medical Practice

Doctor Abel practiced in Brooklyn, New York City, for 64 years. Every day, he walked into his consulting room where the certificates hung on the walls, and was greeted with a smile by Olive his Secretary behind the glass partition. Every day he put on his white coat and visited his patients in hospital, carefully writing the prescriptions on their records. He exchanged congenial remarks with his colleagues in the white hospital corridors lined by the photographs of the ladies who served on the Auxiliary Committee. He attended the Board Meeting in the panelled room with the chandeliers every month for half a century.

Reading Dr. Abel's obituary when he died at the age of 87, I asked myself the obvious question: "Was he addicted to medical practice?" Was he unable to alter his occupation, his habits, his image? Could he have exchanged medical practice for other activities?

The word "retire" and the concept of "retirement" mistakenly implies withdrawal, and giving up something, including our status in society. The more fundamental implication is that stopping one activity allows for a transfer of skills from one set of activities to another, and that it is therefore an opportunity to widen rather than to narrow life.

This transfer of energy and interests, however, requires flexibility and a shift of emotions. Fear of change and unwillingness to look at life from a new perspective is a characteristic of dependence or addiction. I might fail at the new job. I cannot do without this or that habit because of the immediate gratification that it gives me. Doctors, therefore, can become dependent on or addicted to medical practice.

Addiction in this context is defined as dependence on a sustenance or a way of life without which the individual feels physiologically deprived and psychologically unhappy. The addicted individual makes sacrifices which affect not only himself or herself but other people particularly their family, and he/she continually excludes other activities in life for the sake of gratifying the addiction.

Alberta was a red-haired, straight-backed woman who played tennis for her school and won chess competitions. Her father was a Major in the Army and the silver cups that she had won riding horseback as a child sat on the grand piano. Alberta quickly sailed through all the medical examinations and became a Consultant in immunology at a distinguished Medical School in the metropolis. Her students admired her, her patients respected her and her colleagues were envious of her rapid rise. Day and night, her scarlet MG sports car was seen in the hospital car park. Her medical publications appeared several times a year.

One sunny June Saturday, Alberta was married at a large church in the fashionable district of town. The following April, her department celebrated the birth of her son. One week after delivery, Alberta addressed a national meeting on her special field of enzyme studies, while her mother was looking after the baby.

Three months later I greeted Alberta in the hospital corridor. I was surprised that she did not smile.

"How are you and your husband and the baby?" I asked.

"Robert walked out last week. He left me a note on the kitchen table. He said he couldn't continue living with me since I seemed to be giving all my energies to my work".

I was very sad because I thought highly of Alberta and her work. She would lose, at least for a time, some of her zest for life both as an individual and as a doctor. We, who so appreciated her work, would all lose. The Greek motto "nothing too much" is disliked by most of us, particularly when young, but it is indeed applicable when juggling loyalties in our activities.

Addiction implies a physiological illness. This differs from a psychological dependence in which the individual is able to observe objectively and to analyze, and then to chose either to continue unchanged or to modify behavior. In the case of practising medicine, dependence is seen as a first step towards addiction. For doctors, dependence can lead to addiction.

How and why does it develop? What are its effects on those who are addicted, and on those other people whose lives are affected?

Does society play into this addiction? And if so, wherein does society both profit and lose from this addiction?

On the negative side, doctors who are dependent upon the admiration and feed-back of patient contact, and upon being always needed, may have a basic power-complex. Also through fear of losing status, they may become "addicted" to medicine and unable to retire and to change occupation. Friends may reinforce their feeling of being useful in society by saying: "it is wonderful to keep going". Personal needs are neglected, and the balance of dependence-independence in the doctor's life is ignored, so that old age will find a troubled physician.

On the positive side, this dependence indicates dedication to medical activity, with whole-hearted involvement, faith in the worth of the occupation, devotion to the duties involved in the profession, and emphasis on parental "looking after people". Consciously or unconsciously, I have experienced these emotions throughout my medical career, and observed the effect in colleagues. It involves sacrificing one's other interests and therefore sacrificing other people in the pursuit of the gratification which that activity brings.

There is evidence of addiction in many of the biographies of esteemed physicians and surgeons, and in the everyday stories that spouses tell of doctors. The sensation of personal fulfillment which physicians can derive from the practice of medicine makes for strong attachment. We may become dependent on the feedback that we receive from contact with our patients. A chain can link us to the individuals, whether sick or well.

There is a difference between our link to the people with whom we have a professional (business) relationship and those with whom we have a personal relationship. A professional or business link is in may ways similar to the link that binds a performer to his or her art and to an anonymous audience.

Addiction of performers to their profession occurs in many fields. A young flutist once said to me:

"I can't stop playing the flute. I am only really happy when I play. Am I addicted to the flute? And if so, is there anything wrong in being addicted?"

I answered: "No, there is nothing wrong. This is what makes you a good flutist."

In the same way, Vladimir Horowitz was addicted to the piano. He was also presumably addicted to the feedback from the audience, choosing to continue to give recitals when he was over the age of 80.

I watched Segovia walk on to the stage as a stooping little old man; but once he started playing he held the audience of young and old spell-bound with his guitar music. Segovia and his audience were hanging on to the musical emotion, feeding in to his craving for immortality.

Rachmaninoff was well aware of his dependence on the shared emotional high that he experienced from recitals all his life. Toscanini depended on his orchestra to give him the emotional food without which he felt deprived and depressed, in the same way that an addict feels deprived when withdrawn from his "fix".

Abraham Twerski, M.D. in his book "*It Happens to Doctors Too*" describes the widespread addiction to alcohol in the medical profession. One may argue that there is a fundamental difference between the "addiction" of doctors to medical practice and addiction to alcohol. (One could think that "addiction" to medical practice indicates zest and a love of life, whereas addiction to alcohol indicates disease, depression and even suicide). However Dr. Twerski, a psychiatrist studying people of all walks of life with alcohol abuse, wrote that: "They generally react to their particular stress by escaping in to chemical oblivion rather than by coping effectively."

It is true that there is a difference between an addiction which causes physical dependence and one that causes psychological dependence. The addiction to medicine or to musical performance illustrates psychological dependence rather than the physiological "addiction" factor. However, the two aspects can never be sharply separated, since for all psychological states there is a corresponding, inevitably related, physical state.

Gratification makes us doctors psychologically (and therefore physiologically) dependent on the feedback that we receive from daily contact with patients. It is as though we were saying: "Please, my dear audience, think me good at SOMETHING! Otherwise my life shrivels up into nothing, and I walk to the grave despondently."

Since as doctors we are intimately watching people walk to the grave almost every day, why are we so deceived by the short-lived and superficial approval of the "crowd"?

Does it matter to us what colleagues and patients think of us professionally, or what they may publish in the news media? The answer is Yes, but to a varying degree. Most people have a strong need for recognition, but how and by whom this recognition is expressed differs between individuals. Some only need recognition from their family and close friends; some from their peers; and some from the anonymous crowd. Some only need to satisfy private, long held desires. When recognition satisfies a doctor, the "addiction" to medicine is less likely to occur. The need for recognition derives from the emotion that my life has worth in-so-far as I am loved by my fellow human beings. In addition I need to be thought of as "special".

Emotions of a Physician

Each profession has its own particular flavor. The flavor of a medical career is the proximity that its practitioners bear to life and to death. Doctors are able to have the feeling that: "I am not only "special", but I may be part one day of the unlocking of some secrets of life and death". Unfortunately medical matters, although they may involve important discoveries, are only short-lived: they rapidly acquire obsolescence. The sea of on-going events destroys our sand castles.

Only "art" seems to be relatively immortal.

Most physicians are too prosaic and too realistic to consider that they are in the business of "art". Medicine was presented as an art in every century except our own, the 20th century. With the shift of categorizing medicine as a science, the idea that those whose life-work is medical practice can become so emotionally involved as to be "addicted" may seem surprising.

The questions arise again: Is medical practice potentially addictive? Are some physicians and surgeons addicted or dependent on this way of life and work? The answer is Yes.

It is, however, a dependence from which we can shake ourselves, and it need not become an addiction without which we feel deprived.

There are alternatives along the road both towards and away from this dependence, so that it does not lead on to the more significant addiction.

The first step is to recognize the danger. Doctors may not be willing to express this emotional attachment, but it exists nonetheless. Probably the most important preventative is to evaluate, on the one hand, the need for close personal relationships, and on the other hand, the satisfaction of professional acquaintances and connections. Which is of greater importance for that individual? Not everybody desires close personal relationships. Also, the emphasis on these two aspects of life may change in the course of a long career. The emotional involvement can shift focus.

With some individuals, the need to have close relationships for both physical and emotional reasons increases with age. Some people are satisfied with being amateurs and achieving personal skills without perfection. Whereas the goal of near-perfection is required when the profession is being judged by the public, goals for private performance are self-made. Happy amateurs can widen their net and obtain emotional satisfaction of a more varied kind. What a relief not to depend on a critical public, but only to be judged by one's own standards and conscience.

CHAPTER 24

Perennial Emotions, Perpetual Learning

Each generation learns for itself and from previous generations; we react, we reject, we accept, we modify, we apply past experiences to our own dilemmas. So what does this book offer the young?

The practice of medicine changes fast, and young doctors have opportunities and face problems which other generations did not encounter. Physicians now experience different epidemics, the danger of violence in hospital, the power of new technologies and machine intervention, criticism of doctor attitudes, paper chase, unrealistic expectations of medical miracles and the importance of education for the public in order for them to choose health.

Certain issues, however, do not change, and this book describes perennial emotions of the medical profession and the raw edges of this particular human activity. I learned much from reading stories of doctors in other times and circumstances; and their different approaches were thought provoking and added to my own experiences. I have shared my emotions with you, the anonymous reader, who can be instrumental in keeping helpful attitudes alive. It is you who can preserve beneficial ideals which are constant and age-old. It is you who will pass on your ideas and experiences to future generations. Here I describe certain lessons that I learned from experience.

The lobster pots stood on the village quay. Every morning the old fishermen walked down the village street and sat on the wooden bench overlooking the sea. Sometimes they talked, sometimes they stared silently out to sea. On a quiet sunny morning the thin-lipped waves rolled over slowly on the beach. The seagulls squawked on the edge of the stream flowing onto the sand. They strutted and pecked in the stream, which ran from the village draining unmentionable sewage. The Cornish villagers think that the sea will cleanse. The seagulls take their pick off the beach.

My mother and I walked up the village street to visit old Mrs. Dingo. In her dark little kitchen, the iron pot stood on the black metal hearth range, and the framed family photographs sat on lace doilies. Mrs. Dingo opened the side door of the hearth range, stoked the coal fire, and Mother and Mrs. Dingo sat down to chat.

"My rheumatics have been bad this year. Doctor says it's my rheumatics. It's now too far for me to walk to the bakery, so I tell my son I'll bake his pasty along with my own."

Every year we visited Mrs. Dingo, and every year it was "my rheumatics" as she moved around her small kitchen, hunched up, going to the cupboard to give me a piece of saffron cake. I would eat silently. I loved her saffron cake.

Mother and I stepped out into the bright sunshine, and as we walked onto the beach, picking up shells, Mother would say to me:

"Mrs. Dingo enjoys ill health." As a child, I don't think I quite believed my mother, but I wish I could tell her now that she taught me a helpful lesson. We react in our own way to ill health.

Many years later, I walked below the skyscrapers of New York that stand with their heads lit by the sun. At their feet, the busy people crowd on the street pavements. The fast walkers zigzag between the elegant women, the delivery men, the fruit peddlers, and the homeless sitting on the sidewalk. Everybody is in the shade, with the skyscrapers alone getting a taste of the bright sun.

Everybody seems like a pebble being churned up in a tumbler. Often I travel beside my companion old lady in an ambulette, with the driver hooting as we sit immobile among the cars wedged in a jam. When we finally arrive at the hospital entrance, it is again a struggle, with the cranes on one side, the trucks on the other, the road drills deafening the cab drivers' shouts, and the old ladies risking death as they maneuver themselves out of the ambulette with the crutches falling onto their shins.

The day gets spent stuck in the traffic jam, sitting on the hospital bench, waiting for the elevator, undressing and dressing up again in the doctor's office, getting the injection and chatting with the secretaries and the nurses.

"You're looking very well today, Mrs. Littlemore". Re-invigorated from the accomplishment, we sit again at the hospital entrance, waiting while the doorman calls for a taxi cab, and the rush hour traffic piles up outside.

Back in her apartment, Mrs. Littlemore settles down by the telephone with a cup of tea.

"What did the doctor say, Martha?" ask the friends on the telephone.

The evening finishes up contentedly with quadruple repetition of what she said to the doctor and what the doctor said to her and what the nurse said to the doctor and what the secretary said about the next appointment. Nowadays, people don't die quietly of cancer; they and their friends live by, with, for and around the cancer story.

Illness can become a kind of occupation, whether temporary or long-term. Some diseases may fill a life-time and many need life-long treatment. Delivery of health care can earn society's respect, both from the patients who seek drug prescriptions rather than education from the specialist, and from those in the health field who feed on the passive dependence of the people they serve.

In all these situations, the underlying need is the relief from fears, which are appropriate or irrational. This is the central theme, and both the doctor and the patient may find it difficult to distinguish between what is appropriate and what is not. We struggle in the complex forest of facts loaded with emotion, and we usually approach a situation with pre-conceived bias, if not prejudice.

The lesson to be learned is how to discover the facts and put them together with the emotions of both the patient and the doctor. Experience teaches me to try to listen to a patient's story in order to assess the solvable problems with factual information, and at the same time to understand my own emotions sufficiently so that I can appreciate "where the patient is coming from."

In most situations, people have vested interests, but these are often hard to own up to and acknowledge.

I learned the lesson of vested interests in a surprising way. For several years I carried out neurological examinations and evaluations of patients applying for disability to the Bureau of Social Service Disability Insurance.

The evaluation and medical report was straightforward and easy for me with the patients who suffered chronic disabling multiple sclerosis or the effects of severe stroke and other significant neurological disorders. The ones who required all my diagnostic skills were the borderline people with, for example, epilepsy poorly controlled, or low back pain associated with work-related injuries, or various other types of chronic pain. I applied my imaginative search and thoughtful appraisal to these problems, assessing the neurological deficit, the past records, the possibilities of rehabilitation with or without a support system, the prognosis, and the social and psychological aspects. In nearly every case I interviewed relatives and friends in the presence of the patient, so as to have a third party viewpoint; the patient always had this option.

When my report indicated that more could be done to improve the patient's situation, the financial benefits of disability might be questioned by the anonymous people at the Bureau in the State Capital. Sometimes following that assessment, disability money was not awarded; the patients then deemed that my report had been influential and obtained a copy of my report from the authorities. They would then litigate to claim more money.

It is difficult for many patients to feel that they are getting "well" or that they can improve their condition when it seems to their financial disadvantage to do so. The prospect of "improvement" from my point of view was not an "improvement" in their eyes. Likewise the officials of the State did not like receiving these reports, because if the patients were categorized as "disabled" the Federal Government paid for them. If, on the other hand, they were candidates for rehabilitation and further services, the State was stuck with the bill. Either way, I was persona non grata. The vested interests of the different parties were paramount. I became unwilling to practice medicine to foster ill-health. This saddened me. I resigned.

I learned from experience that as doctors we need to accept personal involvement with patients and listen to our emotions but not to over-react. If we are over-ambitious in our single-mindedness, we risk becoming casualties in the deep waters of emotional involvement, our own or our patients'. Commitment to the field of medicine motivates us as doctors, and this ideal keeps us alive. However experience teaches us to balance this with the investment of our time and involvement in family and personal life.

Dr. Bird in his eighties was revered in our hospital, and I admired his energy and enthusiasm. His quick and lively step could be heard in the corridor, and he was beloved by his patients of three generations. As a proud father, he often talked cheerfully to me of his son who was a neurologist in New York city.

One dark December day, my husband and I visited Dr. and Mrs. Bird to offer condolences for the death of this son who had taken his own life. Mrs. Bird sat quietly with a tabby cat purring on her lap. Photographs of a small boy were on the piano; cushions were neatly placed on the empty chairs. Politely I followed Mrs. Bird into her kitchen to carry the cookies. She suddenly turned to me and exclaimed fiercely:

"My husband was never home when the kid was growing up. He never knew what was going on. He spent all his time with the patients."

Emotions of a Physician

My heart ached for the man who felt he was doing his professional best, and for his spouse who was excluded.

In a much less serious situation, I learned the danger of thinking my work so important that it justified the exclusion of other occupations.

I was starting a new job in a Midwest medical institution. My enthusiasm kept me in the laboratory night and morning, making discoveries which I thought at the time were important but which had a transient life like everything else. I expected my team to be equally enthusiastic, and also work long hours.

One day the personnel officer called me into his office. He informed me that complaints had come to him because I expected too much of juniors and they were discontented. I felt a chill of disappointment run down the spine. I accepted the criticism regretfully and learned that one can not impose one's goals on others. While gaining medical experience, I hope I learned to accept criticism. Regrets erode the quality of life, and the attitude of "if only" helps no one.

There is another role that doctors play: that of buffering. They act as buffers between the patient and the patient's reaction to his or her illness and sadness. This buffering role requires imagination.

Elderly Professor Durant, a philosopher, lived alone with his dachshund. The Professor was one of Doctor Blau's closest companions, and they regularly played chess together. When the little dog fell ill, Professor Durant sat up for seven nights with him. At the end of the week he was devastated by the dog's death; he would talk of nothing else and refused to play chess. Doctor Blau, unable to replace the dog, grew tired of hearing of his friend's "irreplaceable" loss, and told him so. He then felt guilty at his own impatience. The doctor found it hard to be the buffer and to treat his friend's depression.

Mrs. Parent, a middle-aged woman, consulted me for headache. She had shielded her alcoholic husband for decades and cleaned toilets to keep the two of them alive. She did not appreciate information which would show that she "preferred" tension headache with financial distress to a struggle facing reality at this stage of her life.

I learned that service to the public does not imply pointing out everyone's "shortcomings".

I was willing to compromise my own values.

We learn in childhood that "it takes all sorts to make a world." We can conclude from this observation that treatment should fit the individual case, and that this comprises the art of medicine. On the other hand, the logical science of medicine suggests differently. We praise those who line up the facts and make the "correct" choice. Although we pay lip service to alternatives and possibilities, we often judge (and sometimes this is in a court of law) that there is a "right" or correct course of action at any particular moment in a medical situation. Ambivalence is less easily understood and accepted.

Doctors study the natural course of diseases, and the progression of health and sickness, written up in textbooks. The variable factor, of course, is the patient. But that variant is too complex to squeeze into a textbook.

And from the individual patient's point of view, it is difficult to accept being put into a category and given a 9-digit number with a social security identity.

As a doctor, I feel that I am primarily called in to be the expert in problem-solving, in fighting the enemy disease or in being the advocate for healthy life-styles. However, I also learned that in certain impossible no-win situations, when the patient is dependent on medical expertise, I the doctor bear the brunt of failure.

The concept and word "case" is applicable in understanding health and disease processes, with percentage chances of this or that outcome. Patients often object to being thought of as "cases". Medicine (and neurology in particular) is not an exercise in botanizing. The work, however, of doctors is to amass knowledge and experience of the "natural history" of health and disease. We are asked to look down the road of life and death and help the patient and family choose the "best" path. Physicians thus have a dual interest, the "case" interest, the problem-solving occupation, and the interest in the patient as a person. The two may go together or they may be separate.

I tried to learn the real skill of a physician, which is to do an excellent job with the "case" and to care for the person while having no particular affinity for that individual, and even to feel antipathetic to the patient's set of values. This requires the "persona" of the physician to play a significant role. When that is so, the patient, while feeling properly attended, is not aware of the doctor's emotions.

The attraction to medicine and the enduring motivation to continue in that profession is problem-solving.

The psychologist Abraham Maslow taught that problem-solving is the fundamental process that satisfies humans. We who practice medicine can endorse this view. We accept the challenge of diagnosis, planning a course of action with the patient within his or her environment, and learning to shape future events with a sense of contentment. The task attracts because of the endless variety of human behavior and of problems confronting doctors. Challenge comes from the differing approaches to problem-solving and from the fact that doctors, patients and their families have different perceptions of a situation.

Mavis was a young woman who consulted me for weakness of the legs. The history suggested one diagnosis, the examination another, the electrically evoked responses a third and the X-rays were normal. I was puzzled and therefore asked Mavis if she would be willing to attend a medical conference so that several colleagues could discuss her case. Mavis at first rejected the idea of being examined in front of unknown doctors. However, when she understood that other brains than mine would help to find the diagnosis and that she was "interesting" to physicians, she went home and announced to her family:

"My doctor thinks I'm an interesting case. She's showing me at a conference tomorrow."

We learn that patients appreciate being considered important, as we all do, and they like to know that time is being spent on their problems.

Patients probably do not think about the doctor's need for them to be "interesting." But I soon realized that for some doctors the continued enthusiasm for their work depends on intellectual curiosity in problem-solving.

On the other hand, I also found that some patients wish their disorder were commonplace and easy to diagnose and treat, and that some doctors appreciate routine work because "keeping up with the times" is so rigorous.

I learned that in certain types of daily clinical practice, for example rehabilitation or terminal situations, the task is to communicate joie de vivre precisely where joy is not evident. This does not imply papering over problems.

I would walk in every morning to the same hospital and meet another newly stroked-out patient, medically similar to yesterday's but with a different personal tragedy. Many doctors open the consulting room door daily to meet a row of expectant people seeking resolution of problems which may be largely psycho-social. The challenge is to be inspired by a recurring problem as well as by a new one.

Intellectual curiosity motivates people in all fields exploring the physical world and human activities. This mental curiosity enables us to work as doctors, year after year, with the zest for acquiring knowledge that we had when we entered the field. We can get up and dress in the morning with the urge to look over the other side of the mountain. But intellectual curiosity may be divorced from understanding emotions, and if it is, there is little contentment.

Experience teaches us that the expression of emotions may be a matter of momentary discretion, self-imposed or socially desirable. It may be an undeveloped quality. Whatever the case, emotional over-involvement generally leads to paralysis of action or inappropriate response.

Thus, over-involvement interferes with the processes of a calm objective diagnostician or the rapid action-operator required in an emergency. The danger, on the other hand, is that detachment as a modus operendum can progressively stultify self-expression in all aspects of the physician's life.

The insidious nature of suppressed emotions may become a longtime habit of shutting-off and of subjugating personal emotions. Stultification of personal self-expression can lead to the deadening of the human spirit or the lessening of the excitement of medicine.

It is difficult for young doctors to be prepared for emotional situations with colleagues and themselves, and education does not teach coping strategies to make meaningful responses. We learn these, however, from experience. Day after day, which pile up into forty years, I listen to stories of patients in distress, stories which they magnify or play down and from which I sort out the significance. This process is routine to medicine. Day after day, whether one feels physically well or emotionally drained, one tries to be on time for schedules, with the pressing need to make a decision NOW as to whether to listen and to act, or to listen a bit longer and to delay what may be rash or effective action.

As a physician, I have spent a lifetime with doctors, sharing their daily chores, their excitement of discoveries that alter the practice of medicine, enjoying giving talks about "our latest findings", appreciating quiet snowy Sundays in libraries, but having to stay in on summer Saturdays to catch up on writing medical records, and on Monday mornings struggling to keep the routine fresh.

When assessing this lifetime, I can say: "It is a good life".

Nevertheless, the sadness of the troubled physician, the anguish of my friends who were the wives with absent or alcoholic husbands, (maybe in the future it will be the other way round), and the daily doctor-bashing in the press and in private sitting-rooms haunt me. Improvement can come from better understanding of our attitudes.

A complex lesson for doctors is to understand, respect and respond to the different ways in which patients and their families react to sickness and to death. It is easiest for doctors to walk away from these reactions. However, since sickness and death of a family member or a friend is in itself a frequent cause of symptoms developing in the near relatives or friends, the issue can not be avoided.

There is no simple answer. Perhaps the only way for an observant doctor to maintain integrity is to walk a tightrope, not repressing personal emotions aroused by sickness and death but not falling for the temptation to catastrophize the situation. If people choose to live by building a pyramid of catastrophe, that is their decision. A doctor can reserve energies for the next problem-solving situation. On the other hand, if tragedy is walled up in a tomb, we must have the courage to explore the entombed emotion. Whatever imaginative response a doctor makes in serious cases, it involves risking personal peace of mind. Experience can teach how to remain involved and intact.

I learned that the ability to listen and to gather data, and to do this with empathy, requires experience.

Hippocrates said that experience is fallacious. I think, however, that if we keep an open mind and take time to digest our own emotions, it is a good teacher.

The most difficult lesson to learn is acceptance of transience. It is an art to enjoy present experiences realizing that we cannot hold on to a magic moment. A physician has the good fortune to encounter many different circumstances and the chance of appreciating a wide variety of personal emotions on the escalator of life.

Bibliography

Alsop, Stewart. *Stay of Execution.* J.B. Lippincott, 1973.

Berne, Eric. *Beyond Games and Scripts.* Ballantine, 1976.

Cushing, Harvey. *The life of Sir William Osler.* Oxford University Press, 1940.

Freeling, Paul and Conrad M. Harris. *The Doctor-Patient Relationship.* Churchill Livingstone, 1984.

Freud, Sigmund. *Psychopathology of Everyday Life.* Pelican Books, 1914.

Griffith, Edward F. *Doctors by themselves.* An anthology compiled by Griffith. Cassell & Co., 1951.

Hayes, Donald M. *Between Doctor and Patient.* Judson Press, Valley Forge, 1977.

Hubback, Judith. *People who do things to each other. Essays in Analytical Psychology.* Chiron Publications, 1988.

Illich, Ivan. *Medical Nemesis.* N.Y. Pantheon Books, 1976

Katz, Jay. *The Silent World Of Doctor and Patient.* Free Press, Macmillan, Inc., New York, 1984.

Lipp, Martin R. *The Bitter Pill: Doctors, Patients and Failed Expectations.* Harper & Row, 1980.

McDonough, MaryLou, compiler. *Poet Physicians. An Anthology of Medical Poetry written by Physicians.* Charles C. Thomas, 1945.

Morantz, R. M., Pomerleau, C. S., and Fenichel C. H. *In Her Own Words.* Yale University Press, 1982.

Nouwen, Henri. The Wounded Healer: Ministry In Contemporary Society. Doubleday, 1972.

Nuland, Sherwin B. *The Biography of Medicine.* Alfred A. Knopf. 1988.

Packard, Vance. *The Pyramid Climbers.* Fawcett Publications, 1962

Patterson, Jane and Lynda Madaras. *The education of Jane Patterson, M.D.* Avon Books, 1983.

Payer, Lynn. *Medicine & Culture.* Henry Holt. New York, 1988.

Pekkanen, John. *Doctors Talk About Themselves.* Delacorte Press, 1988.

Pinner, Max and Benjamin F. Miller. *When Doctors Are Patients.* W. W. Norton & Co., 1952.

Rycroft, Charles. *Anxiety and Neurosis.* Brunner-Mazel, 1990.

Selzer, Richard. Mortal Lessons. *A Touchstone Book.* Simon & Schuster, New York, 1974.

Selzer, Richard. *Taking The World In For Repairs.* Penguin Books, 1986.

Siegel, Bernard. *Love, Medicine and Miracles.* Harper and Row, 1986.

Emotions of a Physician

Slavitt, David R. *Physicians Observed.* Doubleday, 1987.

Smolan, Rick; Moffitt, Phillip; Coles, Robert; and Flaste, Richard. *Medicine's Great Journey, One Hundred Years of Healing.* Bullfinch Press, 1992.

Stein, Howard F. *The Psychodynamics of Medical Practice.* University of California Press, 1985.

Storr, Anthony. *Human destructiveness.* Ballantine Books, 1991.

Twerski, Abraham J. *It Happens to Doctors Too.* Hazelden Foundation, 1982.

Index

Addiction to medical practice, 10, 194-201

Admiration, mutual doctor/ patient clubs, 168

Aggression, 83, 85

Aloneness, acceptable with sublimation, 74

Ambition, control of & strategy, 89

Anger, displaced, 38

Antagonism, responsibility to accept, 29

Antipathy, to a patient's values, 210

Anxiety, 26, 58-64, 139, 181

Attitude, influencing outcome, 107

Autopsy & pathology, feelings aroused, 23

Bitterness, 91, 98

Blending of person and persona, 144

Busyness, constant, a ploy by some, 56

Change, its many emotional results, 91, 95

Competitiveness, 80-89

Complexities of life, inadequate preparation for, 173

Compromise, of one's values, for the patient's need, 209

Compromise, sharing out loyalties, 149

Confidence, necessity of, 117

Curiosity for the new and startling, 98

Curiosity, intellectual, 108

Death, 1, 3-4, 7-8,111

Demands of home vs. patients, 55, 70-75

Denial, 10

Dependence on patients and vice versa, 160-168, 197-198

Desires, to win, to be first, 84

Devotion to patients, 5

Devotion to the profession, 197

Disappointment, 92

Distraction, at illness causation problems, 146-148

Doubtfulness, at being all things to all patients, 190

Emotional blending of medical and life situations, 144

Emotions of doctor & patient mixed, understood, controlled, 205-207

Enjoyment of improvement by patients, 144

Excitement, 93, 96

Expectations, unrealistic, 37, 201

Expression of desires, 75

Failure, acceptance with dignity, 91

Failure, feelings of, when patient discards advice, 178-181

Fatigue, physical and attitudinal, 188

Fear, 27, 165, 172, 202

Feelings of need for praise & recognition, 168

Frustration, at rejection of advice, 180, 181

Fulfillment, sense of, 197

Gender awareness, doctor/ patient, 140

Generosity, needed, scarcity of, 98

Gratification, immediate, 103-113

Gratification, more slowly, 114

Gratitude, earnable from juniors in hierarchies, 57

Hidden disorders, 25, 68, 193

Home vs. lure of discovery, 98

Home vs. work, 70-75, 208

Honesty, the perils of, 68

Icarus, overconfidence, 3

Illness, when it's the doctor's, 143

Illusions, benefits of, 74

Imagination, need for, 54, 164, 183

Impaired physicians, 30

Impatience for instant results, 111-112

Importance of one's job, exaggerating it, 208

Infant omnipotence, 115-116

Insecurity, vicarious, 107

Insomnia, 26

Inspiration, need for, independent of patients, 167

Involvement, in patient social problems, 190-191

Involvement, vs. objectivity, vs. dangers of detachment, 213-214

Irony, 98

Jealousy, 98

Justice— feelings, realities, perception, 169-176

Listening, resistance to, 184

Loneliness, see Aloneness

Loyalty, in hierarchies, 52

Lure of making discoveries, 92, 98, 100-108

Manipulators and manipulatees,

Marriage partners, sharing emotions with, 74

Motivation, changes in, 21

Motivation, sources of, 74, 80-89, 84, 100-108, 211-212

Non-aggression, benefits of, 88

Nursing, 16

Observation, as educator, 52

Overconfidence, Icarus, 3

Pain in learning to accept criticism, 208

Pain of discarding old ideas, 92

Parental role, mutual need for, 42, 43

Passion to conquer a disease, 188

Passionate arguments, 85, 95

Pathology & autopsy, feelings aroused, 23

Patience taught doctors by patients, 107-108

Patient complaints, insufficient time with doctor, 2

Personal traits of doctors, the revealing of, 52-53

Petulance, related to infant omnipotence, 118

Power complex, 196

Power shared with patient & relatives, 117

Power, sense of, both scary & gratifying, 116

Power, sense of, dangerous & fallible, 107

Praise and recognition, need for, 168

Prejudice, pre-existing attitudes, 173

Prestige, effect on doctor's persona, 144

Pride, 96, 103

Problem-solving, a fundamental urge, 211

Professional vs. private life conflicts, 50, 70-75, 208

Psychological states, 199

Resentment, resisting feelings of, 179

Resistance to change, 98

Resistance to demands, 55

Resistance to sharing feelings with spouse, 74

Responsibility, 26

Rigidity, 9

Sadness, acceptance, 40

Sadness, resisting transfer of it to patient, 37

Sadness, sharing, 38

Satisfaction, 65-73

Self examination, lack of visible immediate reward, 173

Self-esteem, inversely related to need of status, 127

Status, the many perceptions, 120-128

Stress disorders in doctors, 30

Sublimation, repertoire of, 70-75

Suicide, 1, 50

Support, feelings and benefits of, in hierarchies, 57

Tension, emotional, 96

Time pressures, 2, 58

Trust, 163

Uncertainty, fear of showing, 47

Vanity, 95

Vested interests, 92

Weakness, fear of showing, 47

Winning, 85-86, 102

Women, attitude toward, 18, 75

Worry, by patient and doctor, 28

About the Author

Mariella Fischer-Williams, M.D., F.R.C.P.Ed.

Dr. Fischer-Williams received her M.D. in Edinburgh, Scotland. After post-graduate work in Edinburgh, and at the National Hospital for Nervous Diseases in London, she practiced neurology in Oxford, England; in Birmingham, England and at The London Hospital, London, where she was Research Associate in the Department of Neurosurgery and Electro-encephalography (EEG). In receipt of Scholarships from the Ciba Foundation and the Welcome Foundation, she carried out neurological research in Marseille, France.

Dr. Fischer-Williams was Assistant Professor of Neurology at Wayne State University in Detroit, Michigan; Research Associate and on the teaching staff at The Mayo Clinic in Rochester, Minnesota; Consulting Neurologist at The Marshfield Clinic, Marshfield, Wisconsin; practising neurologist in Milwaukee, Wisconsin and Director of the Dept. of Clinical Neurophysiology at Trinity Memorial Hospital, Milwaukee, Wisconsin.

Dr. Fischer-Williams is currently focusing on the medical problems of musicians. With colleagues she has founded the Health Association for Performing Artists, and gives seminars on the prevention of occupational disorders of musicians.

Dr. Fischer-Williams has authored four books and 70 papers, including numerous chapters in textbooks. She is the senior author of *A Textbook of Biological Feedback*, Human Sciences Press (1981, paperback 1987) with A.J. Nigl, Ph.D.. and D.L. Sovine, M.D.

Her research included clinical work with epilepsy, EEG, multiple sclerosis, acute stroke and biofeedback, and animal research with cats, monkeys and baboons in experimental epilepsy and evoked responses.

Dr. Fischer-Williams is a Fellow of the Royal College of Physicians, Edinburgh. She is a member of the American Academy of Neurology, the Wisconsin Neurological Society and Wisconsin Women in Medicine. She is Past-President of the Central Association of Electro-encephalographers and was a Council Member of the American EEG Society. She belongs to the Association of Medical Advisors to British Orchestras and serves on the education committee of the Performing Arts Medicine Association in the U.S.

She lives in Milwaukee with her husband, where she enjoys playing the piano and violin in orchestras and chamber music groups.